The Before Trilogy **Ethan Hawke & Me**

Published by Barrelhouse Books
Baltimore, MD

www.barrelhousemag.com

Published in the United States of America

ISBN 13: 979-8-9850089-4-4

First Edition

Cover design: Shanna Compton
Cover art: Circles Trilogy, 2025, Shanna Compton
Page design: Adam Robinson
Series editor: Mike Ingram

THE BEFORE TRILOGY

ETHAN HAWKE & ME

Andrew Bertaina

BARRELHOUSE BOOKS
FOR WHAT IT'S WORTH

CONTENTS

THE BEFORE TRILOGY

Ethan Hawke & Me

Love. I hoped it would happen on a train sometime during my early 20s as the countryside rolled past—cows lowing in the fields, clothes dancing on lines, a murmuration of starlings patterning the sky. I'd pause in my reading and scribble a few lines in a spiral-bound notebook, trying to fit the capacious day into something short, precise, poetic, a rendering of consciousness. But I wouldn't be fully immersed. Instead, I'd be performing a self, trying to find *you* to join with my *I*.

So, when I looked up from my journal, gazing into the middle distance, as I always do when I'm thinking hard, I'd catch the eye of a woman—pretty, probably French. From there we'd play the cat and mouse game of exchanging glances until one of us, hopefully her, because I was petrified of the opposite sex, would open the doorway into conversation. And we'd talk for hours on the train about the way we were brought up, our failures, our antipathies, our kittens and dreams from when we were children, our fealty to everything that moved us deeply—solitary car trips with music blaring, montages of marriages, the death of our first pets. We'd talk about God, absence, infinity, the way our mothers read us to sleep and kissed our foreheads. Through conversation, we'd begin to bind ourselves together, as needle to thread.

But where did that idea come from? A stranger, a long conversation on a train. It came from a movie. I was a child of the nineties, after all.

I've always loved the movie *Before Sunrise* and its sequels, *Before Sunset* and *Before Midnight*. They'd long served as a manifesto of being. So, when I started a new relationship at forty, at the comet's tail of my midlife crisis, I wanted to introduce L, my new girlfriend, now wife, to the trilogy. Back then, we only had one night a week to meet, our little scrim of time, Tuesdays of wine and chocolate and conversation. The rest of the days were taken up with work, with groceries, but mostly with children, two of them for each of us from our previous marriages. *Failed marriages* by that old Christian adage we'd both grown up with and which we knew our mothers still subscribed to. But those failures had brought children, who were not, quite obviously, failures, but illuminations. Constant paradox.

I drive out of D.C. after work along Rock Creek, the slender reed of water that cuts through the city, through the browning deciduous trees, leaf scatter and hills, and onto the large highways into Virginia, making my way toward L, toward our Tuesday rendezvous, bending off the freeway onto the two-lane highway, past a strip mall, before turning toward her apartment and, finally, parking in the small spot allotted for visitors. Through the winter darkness, a square of grass and cherry trees—trees which will be filled with delicate blossoms come spring, and which my own two children will be climbing.

I close the car door, hustle quickly through the misty rain. I've sworn off umbrellas because I always lose them within a week. Up the wooden stairs and orange carpet. A moment to collect myself at the door. Then the rap of knuckles on the white door. The moment of tension before she opens it. We are still so new at this.

A kiss in the doorway and then we spring into conversation, our work and days, making the most of the time allotted, the revelation of self, an hourglass. Only so much time to eat dinner and watch a movie. Only so much time to talk about our *failed marriages*.

In my previous relationship, my longtime girlfriend had found my attachment to the Before trilogy annoying, a sign of my instability. If I identified with the character in *Before Sunrise*—brash, intelligent, a dreamer of all the lives he isn't living—then it was a bad sign, a deficiency in me. And it had stung me, lover of these movies since the age of fifteen. Did I identify with him? Certainly. Was it bad? I'd never thought so.

And now I've suggested that L and I watch the movies, the vestiges of that last sting still swirling in my mind as dust motes in a geometry of light through the window. Will L like it? Or will she develop an elaborate theory of my imperfections? Something upon which to base our future breakup?

I always knew. He loved those damn movies. Yes. With the pseudo-intellectual who never really loved his wife. You know how that type of man is.

Then again, I think, as I pour us both a large glass of red wine, I've been growing confident of late, trusting myself more than I ever have before. A midlife crisis and bottoming out will do wonders. It just takes hours of meditation, legs crossed on the cushion, lots of walks through the forest, river and fall leaves, a few good cries, hours of reading books with titles like *When Things Fall Apart.* The daily walks, birdsong, and the light on the river reminding me that everything changes, everything passes, even this season of sadness.

And so, I sit down on the couch with renewed excitement. To hell with judgement. To hell with breakups. Besides, we have wine, the great equalizer.

I set our glasses of wine down on L's coffee table, pushing aside the beads, books, dolls, and other detritus that always covers it, evidence of a life we aren't yet sharing but one I understand. I have two children of my own, and I've found after months of dating that other parents are the only ones who understand me. Only other parents understand that you're only free for a few hours on Tuesday, or every other Friday between 5:00 and 9:00. Only they understand how much of selfhood is poured into the children, into the fixing of dinners, the wrangling at bathtime, the conversations about death before bed with a being you have seen in their first moments in the world.

Yes yes. Everyone dies. Even you. Even me.

How long does it last? Daddy.

I don't know. A very long time.

Does it last forever?

Shh… you need sleep.

We know how stretched thin we are. Thus, the wine and talk, an island of magical time. And now the movie I've been telling her about, *Before Sunrise*. Once more then into the breach of self, into disclosure, dreams, dislikes, dating stories, old lovers. Conversation is the nectar of being.

I hope you like it, I say, raising my glass.

We toast.

I hit play.

I first watched *Before Sunrise* at fifteen, young and impressionable, learning about a world I didn't know: profound, intellectual, seeking, East Coast. Back then, in suburban California, growing up lower middle class after a brush with actual poverty, the movie represented an identity I had never seen before. Intelligence. Beauty. Travel. An existence I'd never been able to articulate but one I yearned for as soon as I saw it.

And now I'm watching it again at forty, still impressionable, still yearning to find the life as an open field that I desired. But now I have L with me, legs crossed, cozy on the couch, an attempt at renewal. In the previous months when I'd been dating, I'd toyed with the idea of never getting married again, toyed with the idea of dating for years, toyed with the idea of traveling to Patagonia on my own, toyed with the idea of becoming a travel writer, a sage. But the truth is, I like being partnered, even if I've often been bad at it.

In those early days, I often told L this. I said I made a wonderful friend, a fun date, and a poor partner. She seemed unphased.

Have another glass of wine. You're fun.

I like being partnered perhaps because, like the characters in *Before Sunrise*, I like talking so much, finding a self in the space with another. I only understand myself through conversation and writing, the rest is a blur. What do I think? I don't know. We'd have to talk about it. And now it's Tuesday, and the movie is starting, the train tracks flowing past on screen. And L is sitting next to me on her blue velvet couch, my arm resting lightly on her knee, all the things beginning at once.

As we watch, I find myself engrossed in *Before Sunrise,* but I'm also watching L, to see if I can detect in her quiet face a smile, a laugh, rapture. Every new relationship has its baggage to unpack, and these movies have always acted like shorthand for me, a keyhole into my psyche. I wonder what L will see through the keyhole, if she'll love Jesse's openness, his humor, his attention to the world of ideas, philosophy, art. Or if she'll call them movies about an affair, movies about unrealistic romantic ideals, or if she'll regard them as I do, nearly perfect works of art that explore the vicissitudes of life, love, and connection, how time changes our perceptions of things, how mutable and unchangeable our personalities are, how contingent.

When the movie ends, I'm pleasantly buzzed. We've finished the bottle of wine and two chocolate bars. But I still don't know what L thinks. Her face is often indecipherable. Where I'm prone to loud music, wild declarations, dancing and effusiveness, she tends toward the soft, the reserved, the small gestures. At that moment, I feel myself still in love with *Before Sunrise*, with the romance, with the way that the passage of time has changed me, and my relationship with the film, but it's retained its magic, the ineffable quality of meaningful art, its ability to continue to speak to us. I turn to her. Our eyes meet.

What did you think?

And in the split second I ask, the slight delay as she considers, her brow lightly furrowed, I build a defense, a series of arguments, an intellectual firmament, a fulminating defense of the main character's flaws. He's a product of Gen X. He's disillusioned. He's just gone through a break-up. He's twenty-three. He read philosophy too young! Probably even Nietzsche.

I loved it.

Really?

Oh yes. It was so good.

Phew. You didn't find the main character annoying?

I loved how excited he was about the world, how he talked about ideas. I can see why you'd relate to him. It's one of the things I like about you. You're never boring.

That's the goal.

And I loved how cute they were and how they didn't end the movie with something happy. It was just the two of them meeting up and then parting ways. But it also made me sad. Did it make you sad?

No. Not really. It feels like life. We don't have any guarantees. Sometimes we meet people for a moment, connect, and then they are gone.

Do they meet again?

Well, it's a trilogy.

Do we meet again?

Next Tuesday.

She smiles. That's one of the things I would learn to love about L, the way she hopes for the best, expects it from the world regardless of disappointment. Our lives haven't been so dissimilar. *A failed marriage.* But she hasn't taken the lesson I have, hasn't trained herself in disappointment, a defense against failures. We're all just passing through. L seems to suggest that we can find comfort in the maelstrom, an anchor.

We talk about our marriages, about the relationships that followed, about God. Our feet tucked neatly underneath us, another bottle of wine.

Do you think you were married too young? she asks.

Yes. But I think anywhere short of about thirty-five is too young to be married.

Me, too.

But then, you don't wish it away, do you? The marriage. Because we have the children. You can't ever wish away those little loves.

Sometimes I do wish it away. The marriage, at least.

I can't bring myself to do it. It all seems connected. The failure is also part of the success. What about what followed?

I moved on too quickly, she said.

Me, too. It was a bit of a disaster. Thank God I started mediating or I'd still be a disaster.

How so?

Just wound up. Unable to sit still. A lot. I didn't even think I was intense until I started dating. Apparently, I am. Enough women told me so. I finally believed it.

You didn't know that already?

I thought I was laid back.

What else have you learned from meditating? Besides that you're a lot.

Learned?

Yes.

Well, it's convinced me that everyone has something inside them, something pure and good, and it's really a matter of uncovering it. I think you can uncover something. I don't believe in God anymore, but I guess I believe in that.

I love that, she says.

We kiss again, make love, and I drive home across the dark ribbon of the Potomac, the bright Lincoln Memorial shining in the distance, and after the bridge, I turn onto Rock Creek Parkway, where the trees are dark shapes in that even greater darkness, the moon, a sliver in the far-away sky, and I think of how I saw *Before Sunrise* that first time, decades ago, and how it opened a romantic gateway to the magic of conversation, a way of sharing and being known I hadn't conceived of. I think about the movie not only as a forty-year-old, but as fifteen, twenty-six, thirty-five, and all the other times I've watched it through the years.

The movies were more than art for me. They were a portal into the future. The characters were seven years older than I was, which meant I could see my imaginary future in their paths, their arguments, their struggles.

Each time I have watched the movies, my circumstances have shifted alongside them. I remember how it felt to watch *Before Midnight* after my first marriage fell apart, noticing how well it captured the ways things can erode over time, swallowed by an avalanche of bills, of schools, of mortgage payments and health insurance claims.

Like Jesse and Celine, I too fell in love, got married, had children, dealt with divorce. After three movies and countless glasses of wine, I felt like I'd showed L something that transcended art: a spiritual biography, the shadow lives of Jesse and Celine, which sometimes felt more real than my own.

That night, I arrive back at my apartment, a waystation for my midlife crisis, a small, sometimes roach-infested place with a petty landlord who critiques my parenting, my too-noisy children. Once, he accused me of feeding opossums with white bread in the back yard, as though I had nothing better to do with my time. I shut off the engine and walk up the cold stone steps and into my apartment, put my keys down on the console table and go into the bedroom. I lie down and hold up my phone, a rectangle of light.

Home safe. Miss you already.

ACT I

Before Sunrise

I grew up in a small valley town of Northern California: golden hillsides, live oaks bent beneath the heat of the valley sun, tract houses and streets so hot you could sometimes smell the tar melting. Outside of our town great buzzards roamed the skies patrolling for carrion, long wings casting shadows over the roads. In the distance, row after row of almond trees, dusty branches swaying in the invisible breeze. In summer, rice fields were burned, and if the winds shifted, the acrid smell would blanket our town.

Northern California is a place time has no interest in. It's almost serene, agricultural, eons away from the tech boom of San Francisco or the glamorous lives displayed on *Beverly Hills 90210.* I had the sense, as many children do, that real things, important things, only happened elsewhere, far beyond the asphalt playgrounds and scorching streets of my youth.

I didn't know what Ivy League schools were or what the point was of politics. We were sheltered. And I spent my time differently than most of my friends, shy and awkward as I was. Most afternoons I played long, immersive role-playing games, like *Shining Force* or *Dark Wizard*, games where you deployed armies, acquired cloaks, built up strong levels of HP after level grinding.

And yet, I also desired a deep connection. I desired love and sharing. This desire for connection, coupled with my shyness, was at its height in Chico, particularly during those formative and terrifying teenage years when desire and despair burn together. On really lonely afternoons, when the rest of the family was out of the house, I'd sing "How Do You Talk to an Angel?" by The Heights and stare at the ceiling while thinking of Leah Kimberly, a girl whose eyes, which looked like the Pacific I wouldn't see until years later, dazzled me.

As I lay on the beige carpet, staring at the ceiling, all I was trying to imagine was the simplest thing: how to start a conversation. Leah, who often chatted with my friend and me at lunch, where we sat against a wall with a large mural of a pioneer family moving through the western landscape we now inhabited, looking like a crazed version of Yosemite Sam. We chomped on our overly salty fries, passed our hands quickly across the cheap pizza pockets, insides spilling on the ground, pigeons bobbing and weaving just beyond us, waiting for the leftovers.

And Leah, golden curly hair, a flash of white teeth. So, she was there, graspable, tangible. And yet, I had no language to approach her. My friend usually joked with her and her friend, Katie, while I nodded enthusiastically, a dumb marionette pulled by the string of my shyness. The girls would try to draw me out, but I kept my answers to a single sentence. Terrified of what I might say. Terrified of the misstep that might come with speaking myself into existence.

Not only was my shyness debilitating, sex was also a problem. My family was religious, and I was an acolyte in the Episcopal church, which meant I woke up early some Sundays, put on an Alb and spent the morning crossing myself and lighting the candles on the altar, my hands shaking at the task. After school, I would head straight into my room and masturbate, hiding myself under blankets. God, I knew, did not approve, and so I was full of shame—about sex, and about my inability to say anything to someone of the opposite sex. I preferred my dragons and mages lined up in perfect formation, casting Blaze Level II.

Thus, while most of my friends were starting to have sex with their girlfriends or at least participating in the sort of hand and mouth stuff that leads to it, I was playing those games and, when I tired of them, raiding my sister's room for rom coms. The good kind. The implausible kind. Movies where Daryl Hannah had fish scales or Kathleen Turner and Michael Douglass sparred in the jungles of Colombia or where Julia Roberts finally got Richard Gere to love her and her uproarious laugh.

I came to understand from these movies that the reason for existence was love. And, when you couple that idea with a romantic disposition like mine, trouble ensues. Life doesn't align with fantasy. Even if Richard Gere calls for you in the end. In fact, this distancing from reality, a tendency to see the world not as it is but how I wished it to be, still troubles me today, fifteen to forty-two.

My sister, two years older, was the keeper of contemporary movies in our house, and I gathered my tastes from her: Christian Slater, *New Kids on the Block*. One summer day, bored and lonely, I searched through an old cardboard box where she kept her movies, quickly discarding *Matchmaker* and *While You Were Sleeping* before I saw the pink cover of *Before Sunrise*, Ethan Hawke as Jesse and Julie Delpy as Celine, arms around one another's waist and neck, eyes locked. What more could a teenage boy want? I flipped on the movie and lay on my bed. Afternoon sunlight beat at the curtains, slowly turning my room into a sauna.

The opening shot is of train tracks, then a slow pan to two strangers, Jesse and Celine, both reading on the train. From there, the strangers meet, of course, for this is the realm of movies, unlike my life. As they talk, we see the connection building. Eventually they get off the train and begin a night of wandering the streets of Vienna, talking about their failed relationships, having their palms read, discussing marriage and the afterlife as they slowly fall into one another's orbit. The movie unfolds through long tracking shots, the two of them walking side by side or sharing a glass of wine.

Before Sunrise is based on director Richard Linklater's experience from a European trip he took in his early twenties, a single night of conversation with a stranger, and the movie unfolds that way, trying to be a mirror to life as it's lived, the quicksilver connection, the way a conversation meanders, surprising, electric. There is nothing else to the movie, no explosions, no surprising twist or turn. Just Vienna, just the night, just the dark Danube, poetry, palm reading. The only threat is daylight and their parting.

I can see now why I was so drawn to the movie. In truth, to this day, there is nothing I'd rather do than walk through a city, sheer buildings, sunlight blinding, a raft of birds overhead, with my wife or a close friend as we talk about our lives, whether we want children, the afterlife, our childhoods, the things we want to change about ourselves, the world. Deep and meaningful relationships are at the core of human experience. In the longest study on happiness, which started in 1932 at Harvard University, relationships are cited as the key driver to longevity and human happiness. The director of the study, Dr Robert Waldinger, says relationships keep us healthier and happier: "People with more robust social connections showed lower rates of diabetes, arthritis, cognitive decline, and other chronic conditions."

There are an array of descriptions for what makes up a self—consciousness, the soul, a series of bacteria, innate biological drives. But I felt, as a teenager, like something was missing from inside me, as though I was a hollow space. But I had feelings! So many feelings. But they weren't attached to a language. For if language constructs the world, creates our shared reality, then I had no way of sharing myself.

I felt this self urgently needed to be known, to be spoken. In *Before Sunrise*, I saw what that speaking might look like, a cojoined language. As the two leads, Jesse and Celine, discussed grandmothers, the afterlife, God and fate, a lonely teenage boy felt himself opening to the world. Beyond the obvious allure of making love to a beautiful foreign woman was the promise of travel, of trains, of knowledge, of sharing a part of self with another person, so they might reflect it back, complicate it, define it. A reason for living.

Or maybe I've gotten it all wrong. The fact is, as much as I dreamed of love while putting dwarves into a really good attack formation against a wizard, I was also thinking about breasts, about nipples, about skin and flesh and kissing and sucking and threesomes and halter tops. I was fifteen, after all. Let me try again.

This essay is an estimate anyway, a reaching back toward a teenager who is now a stranger to me. I have forgotten so many afternoons, so many crushes on girls with dimples, with little backpacks, so many stuffed animals, my friend Charlie's middle name and almost every book I've ever read. What I'm left with are impressions, as a footstep on leaves in fall, of those things that have shaped me and which tenaciously hold to memory.

A rush of images arise from childhood, those early teenage years, Tom Hanks swimming through the sea in *Splash* kicking his way toward that implausible city beneath the Hudson, mother reading to us from *The Hobbit, The Lion the Witch and the Wardrobe*, our church singing *Silent Night* in near darkness as we leave the service at midnight, holy, Olivia Hussey leaning over the railing in *Romeo and Juliet*, those lonely mornings I stood with my basketball tucked against my hip, waiting for the chain link fence at school to open.

But mostly I think of *Before Sunrise* again, the way it twinned language and desire. And desire was so rich, the texture of it, a flash of skin, of a smile, my balled-up sock, the heat in my room while I touched myself, sex structured all my waking hours. And yet I remained at a distance from it, unable to speak it as trying to speak across a thick pane of glass.

But the movie, which I saw months after Leah had stopped talking to me, gave me a visual vocabulary. I wanted a chance meeting, picturesque architectures, the Danube threading through the bridges, poets on the river. Sex. Sex in a foreign city with a foreign woman who could talk about poetry, and the afterlife, and past lovers.

I didn't know much about poetry, had no lovers, and had never traveled, but it didn't matter. I knew what I needed. But I was still trapped in my town, still shy and ridiculous. I never found anyone like Celine. No one willing to discuss the existential thoughts running through my head, hidden from view. We spent our time enraptured with crushes, who would ask who to the dance, scores on math tests, SAT prep. At lunch, my friends and I piled into a car, listened to Outkast, ate at cheap fast-food restaurants. They had girlfriends. They had people they loved. I had *Dark Wizard* and desire.

Maybe this is just the province of being a teenager, loneliness, dreaming and waiting on real life to begin. A new place to define oneself against. An old cliché about the narrow confines of small towns, the acrid smell of the fields burning miles away, white birds sunning themselves, all else, distant.

Jesse and Celine wander through Vienna after leaving the train, their bodies slowly inclining toward one another as flowers to light. Their romance begins to blossom as they talk, moving from train to tram car, to the streets, all the while sharing their ideas about their lives, his parents' divorce, her parents' marriage, the relationship of his that's just ended, her boyfriend. The movie is all conversation, all discovery. It was unlike the movies I'd grown up on, which relied on contingency, a chance meet-up, a three-minute conversation to establish love. The romance in *Before Sunrise* is built through the act of self-revelation, through vulnerability, through exploration. This was no meeting a mermaid, this was meeting another human being. It enthralled me. To be known.

My mother says, "All that we really desire in life is to be fully known, and fully loved."

Ah. That contrast again. A kind of paradox. How can a person know themselves enough to share it with someone else? If personality, or hell, maybe just mine, feels contingent, dependent on the way another person responds to me, draws me out, then how can you reveal yourself to another person? Isn't it they who are revealing yourself to you?

Richard Linklater, the great American director of the trilogy and of *Dazed and Confused*, is a master of patience, of letting lives develop slowly on screen. His movies work indirectly, more about how two characters glance at one another, how their shoulders almost touch, how their eyes almost meet. This gives his movies a lush feel, something sumptuous, neo-real.

That said, it comes at the expense of the grander shots we associate with movies that take place in a city as lovely as Vienna. The majestic towers, buildings and monuments are largely absent in Linklater's film. Instead, the camera angles are tight, following Celine and Jesse as they walk the streets. The viewer sees bits of the Danube, a street lamp, a corner bench hidden on the cobblestones. The visual texture is not accidental, though. Rather, the film expertly mimics the situation of the characters, two strangers traversing an unknown city as they explore it and one another—the way an avenue opens onto the river, the way a tree sways in the wind, the way a wine shop appears on a corner, the way a joke turns into a revelation, into a memory from a distant country. Each turn in the city, each turn in conversation, a new space opens.

As the two walk and chat, Celine reveals she has been to Vienna before, ten years earlier. They stop in the Cemetery of the No Name, and she searches for a grave, one that made an impact on her as a child. She says she still remembers the grave, that of a thirteen-year-old girl, since she herself was thirteen when she saw it. And now, she says, time passing, she's older than the girl ever was. Her brow wrinkles as she talks, tries to make sense of what's happening, the passage of time, of spaces overlaid with meaning.

As I write this essay, I try to conjure what my fifteen-year-old self might have been thinking, when a song could send me spiraling into a deep longing, a smile from a girl could send a flush through my cheeks, a heat from head to toe. Emotions roared in me throughout those years, dammed up by my shyness.

It was during those years preceding fifteen that I later learned my mother considered sending me to my father's house because she found me so unmanageable. I was so moody, so prone to explosions. I felt, as every teen feels, that no one understood me. I felt a universe inside.

At fifteen, I was starting to come out of that teenage malaise, I was beginning to look outward again, and *Before Sunrise* was a doorway filled with light. I was embarrassed of how much it moved me, how much I wanted to be exactly like Ethan Hawke, handsome, funny, charming, easily picking up an attractive woman on a train. But more than that, I felt like the movie washed over me as a wave of knowing. I didn't know two people could actually try to bridge the gap between self and other. Conversation, a bridge over the Danube.

I don't think I could have articulated that then. In fact, it's possible I'm conflating times now, conflating selves. But I do remember those credits rolling, the afternoon turning into early evening, my room slowly warming as the sun moved west. I remember thinking that I wanted to watch it over and over, to let it become a part of me, to make it real.

Jesse and Celine have their first conflict after she has her palm read by an old woman who offers to read their fortune while they sit at an outdoor café. Celine watches, rapt at the story woven for her by the fortune teller. Jesse pushes his chair slightly back from the table, smirking along at the series of generalities. When the fortune teller leaves, Jesse makes fun of the fortune, insists it's all crap. Celine chastises Jesse, accusing him of being a little boy who isn't getting enough attention.

Maybe I, too, was just a boy who didn't like that I didn't get enough attention. Maybe it's not so much that I didn't know what to desire, but that I wasn't desired. No one was interested in reading me at all. Part of what I would have loved was the suggestion that it was possible to talk to a stranger, particularly of the opposite sex. For it was sex that made it so hard, desire. The plainness of it. I couldn't get myself over the hump, so to speak.

The first argument in *Before Sunrise* is a way of showing how Jesse and Celine differ. She believes in magic, in big changes to the world, and Jesse is more skeptical, a classic realist. But she chides him a bit, calls him a spoiled boy, annoyed because he isn't getting attention. Aren't we all? Attention, Simone Weil said, is the "purest form of generosity."

I remember Celine saying that if there was "any kind of magic in this world, it must be in the attempt of understanding someone, sharing something." And even now, at forty-two, those lines hit me, the same as they might have at fifteen. The suggestion that there was a pathway to getting out all of those roiling feelings, to solving the problem of the self, to solving the problem of an absent God, and it could be found in the space she was describing.

Early in the movie, after Jesse and Celine have just met, Jesse describes a vivid memory from childhood. He, very young, spraying an arc of water with the hose, and then suddenly, his recently deceased great grandmother appeared in the mist. He says he watched her in the mist, comforted. Back inside the house, Jesse's parents tell him he couldn't have seen his great grandmother, that death is final. And he says it paused him, hearing this, to discover ambiguity, even in death.

As I watched the film for the umpteenth time this year, I marveled at the smoothness of Celine's face, the softness of her pale pink lips. I time traveled, too, living at both fifteen and forty-two. I don't think I found her attractive as a fifteen-year-old, her hair and skin were too pale. And at fifteen, twenty-three looked like thirty to me, impossibly old. Now I'm struck by the dueling time capsule, Celine's face on the train, unchanged across the span of twenty-seven years, while mine is hollowed by the creep of middle age. Celine in the cemetery, thirteen and twenty-three.

I find time merging as I muse on her face, smooth, not ghostly, but beautiful. And I think how ambiguous everything is: time, age, perception of beauty. Am I a teen watching Celine, dreaming of the future, a young married man watching it with his pale, blond wife, or a middle-aged man watching Celine in that same moment, with all those moments overlaid on one another as a fresco in an old church? Who's to say which is the true image?

Truffaut says that only true works of art feel fresh with each encounter. A Dutch study revealed that repeated encounters with paintings only deepened the appreciation when the art was of a high quality. Low quality art eventually bores us. It's how I have always felt about *Before Sunrise*, which deepens each time I watch it. Heraclitus said, ages ago, "No man steps in the same river twice, for it is not the same river, and he is not the same man."

Of course, as Heraclitus says, even if the film remains the same, I shift. I have a girlfriend, and then a wife. I have a child, get a divorce, move to a small, dingy apartment. I change jobs, change lovers, marry again. But beyond that, the social mores shift as well, Jesse's jeans appear absurdly baggie, Celine's tiny purse, a relic of the 90's. And the tumbling and shifting of gender dynamics, of the environmental movement, the eddy and flow of identity and class structures, which changes the way we understand a movie even as the movie remains as unchanged as Celine's face.

This seeming paradox, a time fixed in amber, which changes endlessly. I am comfortable in such paradoxes, which are central to holding steady in the flow of time. We are all mysteries floating through a vast constellation of unaccountable darkness, which stretches on either side of our lives. The mystery is that we are here at all.

I try to be a good critic, think through how the contemporary lens shifts the way I perceive *Before Sunrise*. For one, in the contemporary era, there is a growing awareness that male depictions of women are far too often clichés of fantastic figures and dazzling smiles, supportive or quirky women who don't make demands on the men, but merely enchant them. Shouldn't I be proud that my era-defining romantic movie was about the gravity of thought, of connection? Celine is just as intellectually sharp as Jesse, and she is less interested in falling in love than in unraveling the world of ideas. This is a movie about equals, intellectual sparring partners, whose ideas, youthfully infused or not, are the core of the film.

The movie has a 100 percent on Rotten Tomatoes, and the trilogy is included in the Criterion Collection, so it can be hard to find a lot of criticism. In many ways, the trilogy is a beloved touchstone for romantics and film lovers alike. But still, I've heard complaints. I've watched the movie with friends who find the Ethan Hawke character overbearing, a sort of scion of what would later become a "mansplainer." In their estimation, he cuts Celine off during their conversations, dismisses her belief in the miraculous, in the palm reading or reincarnation. He too quickly has answers, dismissals, theories for everything. He's the sort of person who's open to the world only through the narrow aperture of his perception.

It's an ungenerous reading of the film, and of Jesse. *Before Sunrise* is less a gender study of masculine norms in the '90s than a portrait of young adult life. And young adults often think they have the answers to the problems of previous generations. Chalk it up to brain development or the brashness of youth, but Jesse isn't a representation of the macho self, merely a reflection of the late-Gen-X mindset: distrusting structures, trying to think of a new way of making his way through the world. And Celine is paired with him in this, contradicting him at times, complicating him, making fun of how he kisses, trying to puzzle out her own world as well.

Roger Ebert, in his 1995 review of the movie, called it "a love affair" for Generation X, and said the movie felt "so much like real life—like a documentary with an invisible camera—that I found myself remembering real conversations I had experienced with more or less the same words." Ebert, like me, sees the movies as about youth, about how much potentiality lies ahead of these characters, whose futures are vast and unknown.

At worst, *Before Sunrise* could be seen as too different from what audiences are used to, too slow, too trusting of its own edifice. Anthony Lane at *The New Yorker* says the film, with its long shots and unfocused conversation, almost risks being boring, but that it neatly elides it by letting the romantic attraction build, by trusting the slow-paced conversation.

"The charm—the midsummer enchantment—never feels forced; it steals up and wins you. A true romance."

If Jesse and Celine are icons of Gen X, they are also icons of a gentler time in movies, when the only real conflict is whether they'll get together. They wind between romance and friendship and debate the merits of sleeping together. The movie is gentle, sensitive. It meanders, like a good conversation, like a life.

I once assigned a movie review in class, and I had a student of mine say Jesse and Celine were one more entrant in the category of generic romantic comedy. Boy meets girl and falls in love. I disagreed, but I didn't let it tank the grade. Instead, I argued with the student in my head. Of course, movies are about the special moments as opposed to the mundane. But it's different because we don't know if they end up together. And besides! Besides! No one has amnesia. No one is a mermaid. No one is cutting through the jungle of Colombia or dating a friend to make their crush jealous. They were talking, sharing, getting at the core of what it means to be alive.

It's not a fantasy, either. It doesn't suggest long-term romantic connection, that the two will be married happily ever after. In fact, it intentionally eschews that view, having the two leads part at the end with no assurance they'll see each other again. The movie ends as it begins, with the two of them apart from one another. It suggests our moments here are brief and then gone, as a meteor passing through the night skies or the face of an absent lover seen briefly in a dream.

My latter two years in high school, I took walks every evening with my mother, the pavement still cooling from the valley's heat, foothills gone orange in the distance. We wandered out toward the cracked ground, the last areas where the valley hadn't been developed, red clay bisected by dirt bikes, depressions in the land where salt gathered and mattresses and discarded parts had been thrown, amber beer bottles glinting dully in the early evening. My mother and I grew close during those last two years I was at home, when I began to open up to her.

Something had shifted after my siblings left for college. I started talking to my mother about all the things I was thinking and feeling, about sports, about love, about my father, about what interested me during the day, and she listened and shared herself.

In a way, I can now see those conversations were the kind I'd always wanted to have with someone. I couldn't have them with my friends, too wrapped up in teenage angst, and I was still scared to talk much with the opposite sex. Instead, I talked to my mother, and I learned the art of conversation, of listening, of sharing, of disclosure as a form of personhood. My mother taught me how to love twice over, first as a single parent and then as a listening adult. And I can still see us: her forty-seven, me seventeen, our shadows elongated across those foothills, building a relationship I hope I have some day with my children.

She listened to me describe my romantic stories, the girl I had a secret crush on but who I was too scared to approach. I told her how I felt, and she told me how once, when she was young, before she'd met my father, she'd passed on opportunities as well. How even now, thirty years later, she sometimes thought about the man she'd met in Arizona, the one who'd wanted her to swim away with him at Lake Havasu. And I could almost see in her eyes the haze of water, the light-dazzled skies, those red cliffs, the life that had been missed.

As we walked in the low depression below the foothills, vultures hovered overhead, the occasional hawk, scanning the tufts of grass for food while I talked to her about my friendships, my aspirations for college and career. For so long I'd wanted to be an athlete, but I'd come up far short. I was in an interim phase, when life felt open, a blue vault of sky. I know now how much of her life had been closed off, first by a difficult childhood, then by divorce and unemployment. She always carried credit card debt. Our only family vacation was a long van ride to Oklahoma. My aspirations were a kind of shadow life for her as well.

As we walked those broad streets, cooling as evening came on, the sun reddening in the west, she told me to keep learning, to keep attending to self, to follow my passions. And as we walked home, I asked about her life, reminded her that she should start dating again once I left the house, that her life would once again be hers. She never took that life, but those conversations were the seam that stitched us back together after the difficulty of my early teenage years.

Patient listening is what I learned from my mother. And, in a way, I felt myself growing older as we talked, getting a window into the adult world that was slowly coming into view, as a city might on a train. My mother had once been a child, too, had once fallen in love. And now here she was, alone, walking these wide suburban streets, our elongated shadows stretching impossibly far. Maybe it's strange to have your mother as your best friend when you're a teenage boy. But I wanted those conversations to last forever.

I'd gotten braces at fourteen, months before I first saw *Before Sunrise*, and I refused to smile in pictures. When I look at them now I appear to be smirking, but really I was hiding my imagined shame. I'd been so high in the latter half of junior high that people had started a rumor that I was gay and girls stopped by my mother's classroom to ask if I was always so quiet. I remember standing on the sidewalk in dappled light, oak leaves swaying overhead, while my friend and I talked to a group of girls. I remember stepping back and forth, back and forth, as a distressed animal in a zoo, my hands shoved firmly into my pockets, and I remember the hot flush in my cheeks, a few mumbled yeses and no's. I remember the terror of fourteen.

On the first day of ninth grade, I was approached by a girl I didn't know, who flashed a smile and said hello. We chatted briefly before she moved on.

Who was that? I asked my friends.

They laughed at me. We'll find out her name. She obviously likes you.

I felt that same rush I'd felt the previous year, but it was slightly attenuated now, and I sometimes thought about the girl, Andrea, who my friends didn't think was cute, and I wanted to run into her on my own. Though I never did, that desire, to close the distance between self and other, had finally started to build.

That year, my friends and I walked to the Safeway for lunch, ate French bread with mustard, tossed pieces of it to the pigeons who bobbed around on the sidewalk. After basketball practice, I walked the two miles home with my best friend, and we chatted about the day, about basketball, about video games, about girls, as we cut through the golden fields of dried grass, the little depressions where water gathered, fields that have been swallowed up now, turned into tract houses, disappearing like most of my memories of that year.

We are not prepared by television, nor the ancients, for love. Dante looks for Beatrice, traveling across the river Styx and into the labyrinths of hell. But she is practically a figment of his imagination, a woman he hasn't seen in ages. If Shakespeare is the great poet, it does not seem from available biographical studies that he writes to his wife, Anne Hathaway. No, when Shakespeare writes in Sonnet 16, "Let me not to the marriage of true minds/Admit impediments. Love is not love/Which alters when it alteration finds/Or bends with the remover to remove/O no! It is an ever fixed mark/That looks on tempests and is never shaken," he speaks not to Anne, but to love itself, the idyllic, the imaginary. We pursue the imaginary love with the zeal of a fanatic.

I remember analyzing Shakespeare's sonnet in the ninth grade, poring over the words as we tried to decipher what a poet from centuries ago meant about the nature of love, and we probably had to memorize it, too, tattoo the words on our hearts to pour out on an AP English quiz, just as the poet must have intended.

Really, the thing I remember most about Shakespeare isn't the plays, nor the language, but the movie we watched in ninth grade, our bodies kinetic with desire as Olivia Hussey, fifteen herself when the movie was made, leaned over the railing, her chest heaving, beauty incarnate. And I remember watching her every movement, an aesthetic marvel to a fourteen-year-old boy, most of the class was gone that day, seeing Phantom of the Opera. And though I sometimes regret never having seen an opera, I still remember the film, remember her vibrant beauty, the railing, the hot crush of desire.

It's hard to not want to capture such small illuminations that constitute a life. It's hard as a teen not to crawl beneath my trundle bed and touch myself. It's hard to live in a body, which shits and eats and comes and can't ever quite belong to the world. All I do when I come home in the afternoons that year is read science fiction books, one book a day, day after day, Rober Asprin, Piers Anthony, R.A. Salvatore, in my overheated room, turning pages as I allow the books' authors to guide me through worlds distant from our own. Sometimes I stumble on a passage that describes breasts or a quick sexual encounter, and thumb down the page. Then I close the door and touch myself while I think furiously of bodies, naked bodies, the things we'd do all day if we let ourselves become animals again.

Time moves swiftly, but not in a singular direction. I inhabit its fullness. A catalogue of days. I think of all the things I'm leaving out, think of childhood, those quiet hours when I'd move baseball cards across the floor in my room, build elaborate fortresses for G.I. Joes to wage wars with plastic dinosaurs and Transformers. This, too, my neo-cortex says, a life. What of the afternoons my best friend and I raced pieces of bark in the gutters, standing outside in the rarest of California rains? Even as adults, he and I still remember those afternoons, two children huddled over small sticks as they make their way through a series of obstacles, the two of us cheering them along while the rain falls, and the sticks dance or get caught on bits of debris until they tumble into the drain. Two boys, destined for divorce and remarriage, of making and remaking themselves, but bent those afternoons in memory to the task of racing makeshift boats.

The brilliance of the *Before* trilogy can be seen by using the kaleidoscopic impact of all three, a dizzying snapshot of lives unfolding through time, accruing complications, divorces, children, bad habits, old arguments. In the first film, Jesse asks Celine to imagine herself in late middle age, bored of her husband, thinking back on all the opportunities she missed, other pathways that could have been explored. I'm one of those guys, Jesse says, grinning at her with his magnetic charm, begging her to follow him into Vienna, into the unknown.

And how I longed to be like him when I was fifteen. How much I wanted to quote W.H. Auden and talk about reincarnation, about the way I felt when I tried to conjure the infinite, how it terrified me, God's Paradise, which I was supposed to believe in. It didn't just boggle the mind, it horrified it. How much I wanted to share the beauty and the terror of life, how I'd once climbed a mimosa tree, thought its branches the pinnacle of the world, how I'd eaten fat blackberries, how I dreamed of anything but our small valley town.

Jesse intimates Celine will always wonder about him if she doesn't get off the train, that life will be a slow succession of days, of thinking about the chances she never took. Of seeing Olivia Hussey and not *Phantom of the Opera*. Of never telling Leah Kimberly how I felt about her. Life as a series of almosts.

Thus, the movie is as much about the opportunities taken as those missed. It reminds me of the psychologist

Adam Phillips, whose great book, *In Praise of the Unlived Life*, explores the shadow life. In a way, *Before Sunrise* acts as a shadow in my own life, a portrayal of a young adulthood I never lived. I never took trains, never went to Europe, never learned to speak a foreign language or made love to a beautiful foreign woman.

Richard Linklater is the great director of time not because of the way he depicts it passing, but because he's had the patience to let it pass—the years between each installment in the *Before* trilogy; or the twelve years he took to film *Boyhood*, which some consider his magnum opus, following the same characters as they age and change. As such, despite the intensity of the films, nothing ever feels rushed. It feels like a life, which always happens too fast for us to comprehend and too slow for us to pay attention to.

When high school ends, I apply to the same college my sister is attending, a small, Christian school in Santa Barbara. I don't yet have any professional aspirations, but I know how much my mother values education, how it helped her to climb out of a potentially difficult life. Besides, I've been amazed when visiting my sister in Santa Barbara: beach volleyball, the long stretch of Pacific, palm trees, girls in bikinis roller blading along the coast. It feels like television in real life.

And so I drive with my mother down that stretch of California on the 101, small highways and rice fields giving way to cows, to eucalyptus, and finally, after five hours, to the blue-green of the Pacific, ultramarine in the distance. I can't remember what my mother and I talked about on that drive. For the first time, the future was expanding, unknown, and though I left my home town still love-stricken, never having kissed anyone, never having been out on a date, at least I was leaving.

In college, I remake my personality overnight. My second night there, I sit on a wooden bench beneath a sliver of moon, talking to Iris, a girl I'd just met, about the music we love, our friendships, God. She tells me about her parents, about her father, a Japanese immigrant, and her recent visit to Okinawa. She is brilliant. She speaks quietly but intensely, and I am more infatuated with her than I have been with anyone in my life. Our vocabulary is that of the movies I'd seen when I was fifteen.

It's during those conversations with Iris, my first nights of college, in the hills of Montecito, warm winds flowing through the foothills, that I realize you can share the universe inside with another person. Every night, I sit on a bench at 11:00 p.m., hoping desperately that Iris will find me. When we meet, we speak for hours, looking out toward the ocean, hidden by the hills, hidden by the darkness. Every night, we look outward as we speak, as though our eyes meeting would break the magical spell of conversation.

Once, she comes by our dorm room and calls down the hallway. My friend, who also has a crush on her, answers, and he suggests they go for a walk. I sit in my room, alone, thinking of her. Years later, I will learn she stopped by that day to see me. And, in a way, I will always carry the memory of her voice that evening, even now, another life not lived.

Weeks pass, and I never speak of my feelings. I sit on the bench less often, and Iris is often absent. Her best friend develops a crush on me, but I have no interest in her. Months later, when I'm dating someone else, someone who was bold enough to ask me out, Iris asks, quietly, why I never said anything. I cannot tell her the truth, that even though I seemed confident on the exterior, beneath was still a well of uncertainty, of terror.

In a way, this rapid shift in college to an outgoing and lovable character is as unaccountable as those childhood memories. Whatever was obscured in high school was suddenly manifest in college. I am no longer tongue-tied or worried about how I'm being perceived, I am funny and strange and confident in myself. I am reborn and renamed, from Andy to Andrew. Within a few months, I've gone from the shy person who no one talks to to the person who knows everyone, who chats with nearly every girl. But it's just chatter, just exploring the world. I can't imagine dating, can't imagine romance.

It's a cliché of Hollywood movies. Our protagonist goes through a period of growth, realizes some inner strength—a new job, a new confidence, a new lover—and things end happily. But my own growth period is so distinct, so rapid, that I cannot understand it, even now. The rapid evolution of self from calcified to bloom. Every good essay should be an attempt at discovery. And it wasn't until the writing of this essay that I realized the groundwork had been laid in those conversations with my mother, the long chats out in the foothills, which taught me to be a self, to revel in conversation.

Every time I tell people I used to be shy they discount it, laugh at the absurdity of the notion. Perhaps I tell so many people about my shyness because I still think of it as the bedrock of my identity, a part of my formative self. That it's no longer true—in fact, quite the opposite—doesn't matter in the slightest. It was once true, and the vestiges remain, a vast loneliness both personal and existential, like an old train track still cutting through the countryside long after the trains have gone.

My junior year I forego the trip most English majors are taking to England to live in a castle and read—a trip Iris is going on—and instead I head to San Francisco, where I spend the semester working as a hospital chaplain at San Francisco General.

The first time I visit a patient's room, accompanied by an older chaplain, Sofia, we are greeted by a huddle of people, a black balloon floating in the hallway. Sofia approaches the family, says she's a chaplain, and asks if they need anything. No, they're all right. They just need to mourn. I stand awkwardly against the wall, in the presence of death, wondering how I'll ever develop a language to encounter this kind of grief.

Over the next few months, I gently guide alcoholics who have lost their memory in prayer. I give the Bible to a man who has come to the hospital from the streets, and help him to read the story of Job, which he identifies with: the misery, the punishment of God. I journal in the small office given over to chaplains, writing up the experience, detailing people's concerns, their ailments, their questions about God. Some of the patients die. Some get better. I lose the shape of my own story while working in the hospital. It's during those months and those visits that I begin to reject the story told to me by my conservative college, that only those who believe rightly—are straight enough, holy enough, pure enough—can be loved by God. I think it has to be more expansive, broader, or else it's no love at all. At night, I write my first poems. By summer, I feel like a pane of glass dropped from a third-story window.

That summer, twenty-one and single, I drink and flirt in bars. I go to work hungover at six in the morning, abandon the good Christian life I've been living in college. No drinking. No smoking. No girls in the room with the door closed. I embrace the shadow life, drinking so much I spend the evening vomiting in the streets or sleeping it off on a friend's couch. Living life at the marrow. Drinking and bullshitting with friends. That summer, I begin to sense a schism within myself, one between the life I'm living and the one I could be.

Back at school, I try to forget the summer. I attend chapel, stop drinking, pray every evening. Most nights, I walk in the darkness, where only a few lamps provide islands of light on the campus, which is thick with trees. Near midnight most evenings, I walk down to the pond, where I can sit and think, listening to the sound of a small fountain. It is there that I first learn how much I also love being alone, being quiet.

That fall, I meet the woman who will soon be my first wife: a blond, playful, and studious woman, tops in her class. Radiant. An interesting conversationalist. For months, I desire her but flirt with her friend instead, too scared to ask for what I want. Luckily, fate intervenes. The friend I've been flirting with gets asked to the formal dance by someone else, so I ask my soon-to-be wife instead. That night after the dance, we drive down to the ocean, and we sit on the long stone wall in front of the Biltmore wall. Our hands graze each other. We talk. The ocean rolls in and out. The moon threads the water. We start to fall for each other all at once.

I remember those heady days of early romance with my first wife, the two of us sitting on the roof of my car watching a meteor shower we'd been told would be the largest we'd see during our brief lifetimes, our bodies carving out space on the hood of the car, flares across the sky, a monument to brevity, beauty, destruction.

Months later, lying underneath the stars on sleeping bags on a warm Mediterranean night, our bodies folded into one another. There was the low hum of the wind moving through the eucalyptus in the distance, and the warmth of our bodies. I had never felt such an electric thrill, such a promise that our lives would meld together.

A few months into our relationship, I take her home to meet my mother. They like each other instantly, and we spend an entire morning aiding my mother in the garden, pulling weeds, hauling mulch. The next morning, I cannot move as my back has seized up, and my mother and new girlfriend tend to me, make quiet jokes at my expense.

That break, we watch *Before Sunrise* together, the monument to my teenage years. I watch it expectantly with my girlfriend, curled up on the same bed where I watched it at fifteen, time overlaid on time. I cannot remember what we said that day, merely that she loved it, too. We were still younger than the people in the movie. We were both romantics. We were in love. That's the truth. Life can only be understood in reverse. The living is such a bright confusion.

Once, on a day I cannot quite place—was it after we were engaged? before?—we drove down the narrow strip of the 101 outside Santa Barbara, the Santa Ynez Mountains on one side, the Pacific on the other. We parked by the railroad tracks in a small patch of gravel and hiked down a sandy path, which threaded through stunted pines and onto the beach. In the distance, the green and blue stretch of water, all ours. We spent the next hour catching waves together, learning when we needed to start paddling furiously to catch the arc of the wave, to follow its slope toward the shore. On a whim, as we caught a wave in together, we reached out our hands and pulled our boards toward one another, kissing as we met, the ocean gliding beneath us.

We were engaged after dating for nine months. Fast. Perhaps too fast. Maybe it was because we were both young and religious. It wasn't unusual for people as young as we were to start planning their life for the next sixty years. Or perhaps it's that I was raised on movies who taught me that love was the culmination of life, and I was eager to summit. Or perhaps it's that young love is always in a rush, always sure of itself, always sure it will last forever.

The intervening months are a blur of planning, of logistics, of wedding flowers and possible venues for the ceremony, for the rehearsal, for wedding photographers, a time when she feels distant from me as she will for much of the marriage when life intervenes, and the parsing of time with work and childcare allows precious little time for connection, which is all I have ever wanted.

Marriage. Family flies from thousands of miles away, knitting together the coasts. My friends seem rowdy in this quiet group, a bit drunken, out of sorts with the life I'm embarking on, good and solid. Though they remember two summers before, watching me dance drunkenly on my own in a downtown bar, the feel of the music and the freedom coursing through me.

On my wedding day, everything turns strange. I feel as though I leave my body for hours and float above the proceedings, watching as though everything that's happening is not real, but the sort of thing I am witnessing in a dream. Disassociation is usually associated with recovery from complex childhood trauma, none of which tracks with my experience that day. I was marrying a person I loved, flower garlands dotted the pews, our vows had been carefully chosen. A sea of faces.

At the reception, my friends disappear to keep drinking at the bar next door. I down two quick glasses of wine, a flush enters my cheeks, and I finally start to feel myself in the crowd. My grandfather ran race tracks, drank whiskey every day in retirement, and my mother was so scared of alcohol that it's only recently that I've started to drink it and feel its power.

So much of my life has been about performing a self, and alcohol helps me inhabit whatever it is I am underneath, fully. I shake hands with strangers, tell jokes. Outside the yacht club where we are married, waves thrash at the boats, lightning forks in the sky, a fierce summer storm, and for a while it feels as though the whole place is a boat lost at sea.

I'd like to say all the signs are there: the distance between self and other, the glasses of wine, the storm. It's cinematic. But I'm only twenty-three. I haven't really failed yet. Because my parents divorced when I was so young, I have no memories of marriage. All I have are the books I've read, and what I've seen in movies. Of course, a wedding should have lightning and thunder and dancing. But then, we have so few movies about the hereafter, which I'm about to crash into. I feel like a character playing the role of myself. I have no one to tell, so we dance, and I drink more. Whatever comes next is a mystery.

Before Sunrise is a movie about potentiality, about the way we think and theorize and imagine our lives might turn out, different from those of our parents, of past generations. It's a movie about two earnest and well-read people theorizing a future. It doesn't have much to say about marriage, about duration, the very things I was about to encounter. There are no toddlers underfoot or mortgage payments to sort. It had the one thing I'd always wanted, the romance of intense connection.

My parents divorced when I was young, and my mother still brings it up whenever I see her. My mother is a kind woman, auburn-haired and pale, a gardener and a pub-lic-school teacher, my best friend for several years into my early twenties, until I started to lose the narrative she'd given me: God, the afterlife, the symmetry of things. Her life seemed so complete, so good. I couldn't square the idea of my loving mother, proud parent of three successful children, with this woman hung up on the particulars of a marriage from decades before. Why couldn't she let it go?

It wasn't until this past year, daft person that I am, that it occurred to me what had happened to my mother. She had been a romantic idealist just as I was, just as Jesse and Celine are, during their night in Vienna. They both attach to one another, holding a single night as the archetype for all future relationships.

My father had been the great love of my mother's life, the measuring stick for romantic relationships. Because she didn't really date after the dissolution of their marriage, the failure became outsized, not just the end of a marriage, but a failure of an ideal, of a particular version of life and self. My mother lived a good life, taking her tract house grass and making blueberry bushes and blackberries and apricot trees. She drank margaritas with friends on Friday nights, raised three children, shepherded them through college and into marriages, moving everyone solidly into the middle class, distant from her own troubled upbringing. But she also gave up on her own dreams, her ideals about love, her desire to become a writer. And my father left. And that became one of the stories that structured her life.

She says, "Your father was already having an affair when you were born. He never intended to raise you."

For most of my early twenties, I viewed my life as a corrective to my father's. I remember the one baseball game my father attended, his presence in the stands as I nervously patted my glove at shortstop. The truth is, I was athletic and good and full of fear. A ball was smacked towards me, low and hard, and I bent at the waist to snatch it, but it took an uneven bounce off the turf, where grass met dirt, and smashed into my shoulder, leaving seam marks cut into flesh.

As tears ran down my face, my coach asked if I was all right, and I shook my head yes, pulling the bill of my cap lower. I had made an error, bad bounce or no. I didn't look at my father who sat on the cold bleachers, avoided his eyes at all costs. Overhead, I saw gnats bumping into one another in halos of light. I patted my glove and waited on the next pitch, shoulder screaming in pain, full of overwhelming shame.

My parents barely talked. We were exchanged a few times a year at a McDonald's in Vacaville, California. A place I can still conjure, peering anxiously for my dad's silver Cadillac, the undeveloped field behind the McDonald's, star thistle and brown grass save the winter months, when it turned a vibrant green and geese V overhead. We often peed in the outdoor bathrooms, briefly got Happy Meals—a misnomer, it's clear—before being shipped away in his car. On the way to San Jose, we crossed over bays, over bridges, looking outside at the blur of land, listening to the hum of the wind coming through my father's perpetually open window, on the way to his house, a place that never felt like home.

When I was a child, I swore I'd never get divorced. I swore I would grow up to become a father to my children, teach them to throw a baseball, tell them routinely that I loved them, snuggle them, read to them, make a solid structure for them to build their lives. It was a response to those long drives, my father saying, "stop crying or I'll give you something to cry about." A response to his absence, to that one baseball game he'd attended where I'd been betrayed by a bad hop, my one chance at salvation, to make my father proud.

Inside every cynic is a disappointed romantic. And for years, I see now, I lived in that cynicism, disappointed that life wasn't more romantic, more fulfilling.

Here's a strange thing about this writing project. It's my third pass through the essay, one that has taken fourteen years, so pieces of the first essay, written at twenty-eight, are still embedded in this one. And it's like an archeological project to uncover them, to look between the layers of sediment and discover previous eras, prior iterations of self. You can find trilobites in the desert, signs of vast inland seas. And so I retain the fragment below, written when I was twenty-eight, as a reminder of that past self, now swept beneath the avalanche of days.

From the earlier essay: "Somewhere between 3:00 and 4:00 a.m. one night, I dreamed I was an artist. I tapped on the keyboard to the sound of traffic and soft rain. Somehow 30 is approaching, and I've done nothing. My mother said I could do anything I put my mind to. And yet I've failed at so much. The lamplight reflects off the glass, which reveals the bookshelf lined by a hundred authors. I try to put my mind to rest, think of the impending move to a house, children, and a yard. The impending realities of life, and I stare at the reflection in the window, gone slimmer in the face, hollower around the eyes.

"Five married years later, and I occasionally ask her to speak Swiss so I can fulfill my dream of being with a foreign woman. If she works hard enough, perhaps we'll have a staged meeting traveling around Europe this summer on a train. And we'll spend the rest of our lives talking about our first day together."

Even then, at twenty-seven, I'd already noticed the German couple fighting at the beginning of *Before Sunrise*, which is the impetus for Jesse and Celine's meeting in the train car. Back then, I looked up the dialogue and discovered that the movie doesn't begin with romance. It begins with an old married couple saying they can't stand each other anymore. I say in that old essay, sounding much older than twenty-seven, "All the stories eventually get told, lines show up in our faces, ideas begin to fade, we forget what we used to dream."

Back then, we'd only been married a few years, but the fracturing had already started. There was a kind of narrative discontinuity that had started to come out during graduate school. She had our lives planned on a carefully made track—savings, house, the occasional vacation when we'd properly budgeted—and I wanted to wander through European cities, pick our way through the streets until we stumbled on squares filled with sculpture and light. She thought it impractical.

We were both right, but I couldn't see it then. In that old excerpt, the long essay I'd written ends by describing her asleep, her hair "fanning on the pillows, her breathing slow and even, that conversation without end." I think what I'd meant to say and perhaps what my classmates had intuited was that the conversation had already ground to a halt. And I'd shown it to them, how can you have a conversation when one person is sleeping, and the other is talking only to themselves?

At the end of *Before Sunrise,* Jesse and Celine part ways. They don't exchange any information for fear of receiving sad emails, long phone calls, losing the magic they have established. But they agree to meet in the same spot in six months. Celine boards her train, and the camera remains with her as she watches the countryside go by, eyes heavy-lidded, until she passes into sleep.

As a fifteen year-old, I was left with a dream of the life to come. When I watch it now, I'm struck by so many things, but mostly the contingency, the fact of how it could not have happened at all. Life is like that, sometimes an opportunity rises before you, then fades, as mist through the arc of water from a hose, as a face passing by on a train.

ACT II

Before Sunset

I saw the second movie with my first wife when it came out in 2004. We were living that first year after marriage in the beach town of Carpinteria. This was back in the years before every cast member and movie project was tweeted about long before it had come to fruition, so *Before Sunset* arrived as an absolute surprise. There was no promise we'd ever see Jesse and Celine on screen again.

I was driving with my wife through the streets of Santa Barbara: palm trees, sunshine, roller bladers, the life I'd once seen at a distance now mine. As we passed the marquis for the small theater, we saw *Before Sunset* listed and cried out in joy and bought tickets to the evening showing. We were so in tune. That evening, we watched the movie, spellbound. When it ended, the audience gasped, then began clapping.

The second movie tracks Celine and Jesse as they wander through another European city, Paris, this time with the weight of nine years tethering them to the real world, which is absent in the first film. If *Before Sunrise* is about the magic meeting of chance, *Before Sunset* is about the consequences of not fully seizing that chance, of having the missed opportunity become more real than life.

The premise is that Jesse has written a book about his night with Celine in Vienna, hoping to find her somehow. As he tours Europe, she finally appears, at his final stop in Paris. It's clear that their brief romance has become a cornerstone for the way he understands his life. When she shows up, he stops mid-sentence, caught by her surprise appearance, stunned and delighted. And over the course of the next eighty minutes, they walk the streets, discussing life, this time as thirty-somethings: wiser, sadder, more in tune with the failed hopes of life than future dreams.

As they walk the cobbled streets, duck into small cafes, pass a cigarette back and forth and talk about climate change, about failed romance, their chemistry slowly builds, and I found myself falling in love with them all over again. The contingency of it, the illumination of their meeting again, the pull of desire, of conversation, of connection. No wonder we all clapped at the end.

After the movie was over, my wife and I drove home, the hum of the car on the highway, the distant ocean, glittering as a snake. As a teen, I'd dreamed of having a beautiful wife with long blond hair and blue eyes, too influenced by television and *Baywatch*. As we drove home, my blond-haired and blue-eyed wife and I, talking about the movie, it was hard to recognize the endless scroll of days that Jesse complained about in the movie, the way a marriage could turn into a prison. We were driving on a strip of road at what felt like the edge of the world. We were still young and full of hope. We were going to drive forever.

Back then, we still got excited to spend time together, to watch a movie, to walk along the beach, where the Pacific crashed into the cliffs, where seal pups huddled against their mothers and oil bubbled up from the ground, mere blocks away from where we lived. Or maybe we weren't excited. It's hard to remember through the haze of time, which tells its own stories, makes up its own endings.

Evenings, we'd walk along the coastline, waves gliding smoothly into the shore, the sky a cathedral of pinks and purples, holding hands and chatting about our lives, our office jobs, our hopes for the future. On Saturdays, after I was done watching football, we'd walk the long trail on the beach and then throw the football back and forth for twenty minutes. I tried to teach her how to swivel her hips, how to use her shoulder to lean into the throw.

But the truth is, I find it hard to remember the emotional tenor of those early days of marriage. That was almost twenty years ago now, and I seem to recall complaining of how the weather in Santa Barbara was always so perfect, bemoaning the fact my then-wife always cheerfully said how nice it was. It's nice every day, I answered, as though that spoiled it. I remember a quiet sort of exhaustion falling over me, a discontent with the pattern of the day, with my job, with the waiting that seemed to be so much a part of adult life, as though, even after we were married, we were just playing at it. I saw myself being a husband. Life as a movie.

I worked nine-hour days, first as an assistant working with elementary school kids, the first year at a lower-income school, where I worked with the slowest readers, haranguing them into reading in a group with me while they made fun of one another, mocking each others' little mistakes and pronunciation errors. I felt depleted, constantly reminding them to get back to the page, to stop tearing each other down. I felt like my time was worthless, wasted, that they weren't learning.

In the afternoons, I made my way across town, taking a brief nap in the park every day. In the distance, I could see the soft edges of the Pacific beyond the grove of evergreens. Then I made my way to an after-school program where I worked on a database, prepared snacks—quesadillas, French fries, grilled cheese sandwiches—for forty kids. When the children arrived, I played basketball, tag, hockey on the cement, and then put on a movie while I waited for the parents to pick them up.

In those days, it was rare that I spoke to anyone within my age range. Day after day, I was talking to children, playing with children. When the one thing I'd always wanted was a real conversation. I doubted myself, began to wonder what sort of career I might find. Though I always found the kids amusing, something was missing, and I felt it, acutely. I had found love. Why was there still desire?

In truth, I think I felt confusion, a distance from the life I was living, which seemed scripted by someone else. I was play-acting at being a self once again. I felt as though I'd had a brief dream during college, a time when my life was finally realized—friends, laughter, romance that had quickly been extinguished by the realities of bills, car payments, rent. If it wasn't a marriage, and it wasn't work, what was the promise of adult life? How long did it stretch out?

And still that might not capture the important thing about that time, which wasn't so much about life but about how I conceived of my life. I can't quite remember how I felt as I lay on the bed, reading Tolstoy, while she prepared veggie burgers on our two-burner stove. How I felt after we bought a couch, which was coated in dog hair, or the hours spent cleaning each individual hair, putting tape on our hands, vacuuming and eventually covering the couch with a sheet. What of the surfboard I bought on a whim and used only twice? The way she told me it had been an impulse buy, and I tried to thwart her, woke up at 5 a.m. on a Saturday, walked to the beach, early morning light, rocks and sea dash, tumbling headlong over the board time and again, water pouring inside my ears, my nose, the ocean inside. Finally, the fear of sharks pulling me back to shore, away from the life I thought I might want.

There were spiders in the corner of our small studio apartment. I read voraciously every evening. These were the months, the books, that would later lead me to imagine I might be a writer. But were we happy then? I can't say. I think we were mostly just young and beautiful.

And then my wife and I hit a breaking point. It was something seemingly minor. My car, a cheap Chevy, had broken down, blown head gasket. It was going to be $900 to fix. I broke the news to her, and she said we'd have to think about it.

Think about it? We have to fix it.

Well, we have to think about whether it's worth it.

I need a car. I can't drive to work in nothing.

But we need to think about whether we can afford it.

I can't afford to not drive to work.

But we need to decide if it's the right thing to do.

What else could we do?

I don't know. Maybe think about buying a new car?

That's more expensive.

I know, but it might be the right thing to do.

After a half hour or so, I realized she wasn't going to break. I wasn't going to get her to agree to what I saw as a simple truth: we needed to fix the car. It wasn't a question. And no matter how much I pressed, how much I complained, she wouldn't see the rightness of my position. We needed to think about it.

Twenty years later, I am still an impatient person. When faced with a decision, a menu, a new car, a vacation, I decide quickly. When I'm asked to wait for a decision, I feel my stomach churn, and my pulse elevate. What the hell are you waiting for? Make the decision and move on. Part of my disposition is backed by social psychology—we tend to justify our decisions after the fact, inclined by confirmation bias to believe in their rightness. But my first wife didn't see it that way. For her, each decision, especially when it came to money, opened up a large decision tree, a branching of possibilities that needed to be considered, agonized over. We needed to draw up lists of pros and cons. We needed to imagine our lives with a fixed car, with only one car, with a new car, with no cars at all. All these possibilities must be embraced before we could make the decision about whether to fix the car or punt it into the sun. It drove me mad with rage.

I stormed out of the house that night in a fury. I took a long walk through the chilly, coastal air. On the street, cars were limned in salt from the ocean breeze, and I unconsciously stalked toward the ocean, mumbling about the rightness of my position. After three blocks, I reached the end of the roads, and I looked out over the train tracks, beyond the stand of Eucalyptus, where the moon was lying like a ribbon on the ocean. I walked over to the cliffs overlooking the ocean, sat on a bench. The infinity of sky; the infinity of ocean.

Our marriage would not be perfect. Perhaps it was broken.

We had been married nine months on the night of that first fight.

And through the veil of time, twenty years out, I can see it was the same fight we'd have for the rest of our marriage:

who gets to decide where the money goes? I would always want to spend it on travel, on meals out, on pursuing the sort of life I'd seen on screen, full of romance, truth, beauty. And she'd always say we needed to think about it first, we needed to consider all the variables, and if we wanted to go on a trip to Spain, name our child, go out to dinner, we needed to save up, consider the costs, make sure we gave her the right name. My incredible impatience. Her incredible stubbornness. Hammering against each other for as long as we could both take it, waves crashing into rock.

We lived there for a year and then she applied to graduate schools across the country. So we left Santa Barbara, the century plants, the flowering cactuses, the blue-green Pacific. We headed to the Midwest so she could start graduate school in Ann Arbor.

It was there, in the cold Midwest, that my romantic ideal of life fractured completely. I worked at a pre-school outside of town, an old house converted into a place for toddlers to pile into one another, to piss and shit and read books and play in the snow.

One child stood out, though, a small boy who threatened his classmates, threw large toy trucks at their heads, chased them with a butter knife. Terrorized everyone. Somehow, I was tasked with "relating" to him. I was taught how to restrain him, pulling his arms over his head and holding him, leaning my head back, so he wouldn't smash my nose as he threw his head back and forth. He sent a fellow teacher to the ER with a bloodied lip.

The staff there trained me with taking care of this troubled child. I sat on the long red walkway outside of the school, the pale sun shining down on the icy steps, talking to him. Trying to keep him calm as we waited for the bus that would take him to a school more suited for a child with his needs. He zoomed around me, talking about *Friday the 13th*, how he'd like to smash everyone with a knife.

No, I said. That's not how we talk about other people. Don't you want to talk about dinosaurs?

No. I want to talk about killing.

And then the wait, the cold, the distant trees, swaying in a northern breeze, branches clacking in the distance.

I drove through the streets, snow piled against the leafless trees, skeletal branches holding the gray, wondering if this was the world I was promised, underpaid and terrified of a child. I wasn't just bemused by life. Instead, life felt as though it would be an unending chain of disappointments.

I left that job, certain I'd go crazy if I didn't. During the second year of my wife's graduate education, I took a job at the university, filing papers for business school applicants, cutting open packages and sorting the materials into Byzantine piles. I worked in near-silence for months. I was a good decade younger than most of my colleagues. At lunch, I'd sometimes walk outside, trying to escape the florescent lights, and eat a small sandwich beneath a leaden sky.

The sun was rare there. I spent my days helping to plan and sort the lives of people who were more successful than I was. I had seen snow once in my life. That winter, it snowed seventy-two inches, and I felt my whole life muffled by its whiteness.

By February of that year, I was fully in a quarter-life crisis. I'd walk home beneath those dim skies, blaring sad music, Ryan Adams begging his friends to take him out, to fuck him up. But I didn't have any friends, or at least not the sort who would get me drunk. There was just the sky and the piles of meaningless work, but I wasn't supposed to say anything.

I had reentered that strange place I'd inhabited in high school, a self amongst strangers who didn't care to know me. Or maybe I just didn't know myself. Maybe I wanted to get drunk and stop believing in God. Maybe I wanted to travel on a cheap budget and sleep in hostels. Maybe I wanted to give up on the life I'd started, find a new track.

We had a small respite in Ann Arbor, our church on Sundays, where I'd glaze over during most of the sermons, the peculiar boredom of being preached to, the sitting and standing, the rituals of worshipping a silent God. But I liked the people there, who were kind and intelligent. The sort of people who, had I not met them in church, I'd have befriended. I already had some vague premonition I no longer thought of God as real, but I could hardly tell that to my pastor over dinner. Or maybe I could have tried. Maybe the great lie I've always told myself is that I'm saving others by not revealing myself, so worried I'll be rejected.

On our best nights, we'd drive across town to the arboretum, where a couple we'd befriended lived. They'd work in the large arboretum, pulling out invasive species, doing controlled burns, and planting on the weekends. We'd join them every now and again for spades, and we'd drink wine, play cards, laugh late into the night. The house was a harbor of light in those endless days of gray.

But still, I had nowhere to turn for my career, which was at a standstill. I remembered those walks from when I was a teenager, my mother telling me I could be anything I wanted. A lie. I couldn't be anything. I would spend my life underemployed, uninspired. I'd never developed a plan, never had an idea of what I was for. I was nothing like my wife, and my mother had told me I could be anything, which turned out to mean nothing.

The previous year, I'd made friends with a fellow teacher, Lydon. We used to hang out during our breaks from the pre-school, standing by our cars, our breath making little pockets of air in front of us, chatting about the dysfunction of the school. She was upbeat and cheerful, while I was hanging on to any semblance of rationality by a thread. Her husband, Eli Vonnegut, was Kurt's grandson. Once, they invited us over for dinner, and after we'd eaten the chicken and had a couple glasses of wine, we started talking about books. I told Eli I'd always loved books, and he spoke glowingly of his grandfather.

What should I read next, I asked him.

Read *Infinite Jest*, he said. It's a doorstop and weird, but I think you'll like it.

I could hardly turn down the recommendation of a Vonnegut, and I spent the next month poring over the pages of *Infinite Jest*, immersing myself in a world that wasn't my dismal, cold life in Michigan. I watched Hal Incandenza play tennis, watched his father microwave his head, the whole nine yards. I fell in love with literature again, with the possibilities of the novel. In *Before Sunset*, Jesse becomes a writer. That year of reading, I thought I might, too.

At the tail end of our time in Ann Arbor, I told my wife I'd like to consider a career in creative writing. I knew nothing. I was as naïve and romantic as I'd always been. I had taken one course in undergrad, where my poetry packet had been given a C+. I turned away from the life I was living, dead-end jobs in education and offices, and fixed my gaze back on the romantic, the life of a writer. I had always wanted to live anywhere but inside my own life, which felt like a trap, and I thought I might have found a way out.

In *Before Sunset*, Jesse begins shyly, his movements are jittery, exuberant and afraid all at once. They missed their meet up nine years earlier and haven't seen each other since. It was Celine who didn't show up to the meeting they'd planned, her beloved grandmother had her funeral that day, and Jesse, played brilliantly by Hawke, manages to convey the fear she'll disappear again if he so much as touches her. Celine is surer than he is. She's had time to consider their meeting. She's read his book. She knows he still thinks of her. Beyond that, Celine knows Jesse is now married, so there is something slightly distant in her, a part of her self is held back, protective.

As they weave through the streets of Paris, they touch on their conversation from nine years ago. They have some of the same talking points, but their perspectives have shifted. This time, Celine says she doesn't believe in reincarnation, but now she fears climate change, imperialism, gun violence. In a way, you see her youthful idealism transmuted into something more practical, an acknowledgement of the world outside a self, a world interested in its own destruction.

Jesse, too, has changed, spent time in a Trappist monastery, developing a quieter sense of being in the world. The youthful cynicism has dissipated some, but he still feels skeptical of the contemporary world, of structures, of marriage and happiness, and of himself. Time passes and perhaps we become more ourselves, habits ingrained, mannerisms sharpened.

For a brief time, writing seems like it will be the refuge I was looking for. I will be able to create, each morning or late at night, a world of my own, with beauty and light and characters who talk about God and class and sadness. My wife, always supportive after thinking things over, helps me apply to MFA programs, and I am waitlisted at San Francisco State and accepted at American University, in D.C. For a while, I think about returning to San Francisco, a city I love. I think about how much I adore California. But she gets a job in D.C., and we're off to make our lives anew, she in the government, me as an aspiring writer.

I begin my MFA excited to read and write those stories. Within months, though, clarity arrives, and my skepticism rears its ugly head. I begin to read the grim statistics about how few people carve out a life from writing. I read my classmates' stories, stand outside while they smoke cigarettes in the dark, listen to them talk about how hard it is to find a fun bar close to campus, how awkward everyone is. A friend, very high, walks out during the critique of my story, wanders the hallways saying hi to papers, and I wonder what we're all paying for around that table.

I had come into the program so naïve. I expected everyone to be in love with books, with Tolstoy and Moby Dick. I used to stand outside of the classes after they'd finished, huddling with my classmates in the cold.

I can't believe how much fucking reading they make us do. Like, I'm not here to read books. I'm here to write. That's why I signed up for this program.

I nodded my head, secretly confused. Wasn't that what had inspired us to write? Other writers? Did they really think they had nothing to learn from Woolf or Faulkner?

I started researching writing, talking to my professors. My professors all seemed to be teaching to supplement the life they really wished they were leading, the writing life. I saw that the pathway I'd chosen wasn't really a career path, it was merely a diversion, the chances of success so scant as to be nil. I started to see that even if I loved it, writing could not be an end in itself. Where to turn next?

It was during these years that I stopped believing in God, but I continued going to church, where I sang hymns and shook hands with everyone I met. Yes! Yes! This is the life I want, I signal to everyone while not wanting it at all, wanting to take a train elsewhere, through a countryside full of still water, white birds, fields of wildflowers. At least the romantics lived in an era of poetry. At least they could write long, flowery letters about the summer garden.

Before Sunset has a less idealistic message than its predecessor. In not meeting Celine, Jesse has allowed his unlived life, based on a single night with her, to consume his real life, which includes marriage and a child. Though he's found professional success with a book, he says his life still feels listless. He confesses to Celine that he wrote the book in hopes of seeing her again. He says he loves his son, but he seems to regard his life and marriage as a prison, less a choice he made than a logical progression of a relationship, two people who used to love each other just raising a child.

If the first movie was intended as a subversion of the romantic tropes of the '90s, the second could be seen as a continuation of an overly idealized love. Certainly, Jesse's obsession with one night should not be allowed to overshadow the years he spent with his wife. However, studies have shown that we listen closest to a person during the first six months we know them, when they are still a mystery to us. After years, the conversation dulls, not by inattention, but by the way our brains are wired.

I remembered the conversations my wife and I used to have in that first blush of love, not the content, but the feeling, as though the whole world was opening. What it felt like to discover someone's thoughts about God, mathematics, *Middlemarch*. And then the conversation starts to lose steam. The perspectives aren't new, they're known. Every conversation can begin to feel like a conversation you've already had.

She is very detail oriented, loves to keep a clean house. She says how happy it makes her to have clean and empty surfaces. I can't understand her. I read books all over the house, leaving them spine down in random places. I carelessly put my dishes down on the coffee table, forgetting myself in a novel, or in a story I'm telling about work. We argue over the dishes and how we spend our time. She likes the house spotless before we leave for an activity, and we sometimes take hours to go out while I grouse on the couch, and she reminds me that I could help. Eventually, she starts doing the dishes silently while I read from a novel, both of us frustrated.

In the movie, amidst the disappointment of a failing marriage, suddenly all those missed opportunities come into sharp focus, a reversal of the scenario Jesse lays out in the first movie. The rekindling of their romance is not only about romantic projection, but also about the fulfillment of the life that didn't take shape when they failed to meet up nine years earlier, a life more real than his own.

My sister, once my romantic gateway to the *Before* series, told me she loathed the second movie. What she loved about the first movie was the romance, the possibility. But the second movie, in her view, is callous and self-involved. It's a movie about an affair.

While that is technically true, the aperture of the movie limits the impact. Once again, the only characters on the screen are Celine and Jesse, which means the audience doesn't have to consider the impact of the affair. Cleverly, his wife is imaginary. We don't have her concerns, the shape of her face, her life, just Jesse's brief monologue. That's why I don't see the movie that way. It feels like a culmination of romance, a deferred chance finally realized.

Everyone knows controlling interpretation is the key to discussing a relationship, a movie, a life. Just as everyone knows the truth is ambiguous, found in the space in between. I want to remind you I can only give you a small picture of things, like a distant mountain, viewed through a rising fog. So much is left out, so many things elided, unknown. I have long said we are mysteries to ourselves, which makes our partners, who we think we know so well, doubly mysterious.

I remember a long drive we took with my then-wife's parents into the mountains of Colorado, where we walked around in a remote valley at ten thousand feet, awed by the waterfalls, the aspen groves, leaves shimmering, the feeling of being somewhere almost untouched. I remember sitting at the edge of the waterfall, as alive as I've ever been. On the drive back down from the mountain, my wife and I sat close together, holding hands, marveling at the bounty of the world.

In graduate school, a friend calls *Before Sunset* the perfect film, from the first moment Jesse spots Celine at his book signing, the shock of presence making its way across his face, until Celine's final lines, "Baby, you are going to miss that flight," the movie somehow inhabits dual spaces, the magical and contingent.

In this view, the second movie is a complex romance. But even within that interpretation of the film, a divergence occurs. For some viewers, the nine years lost are what stand out, the flowering of their romance missed because Celine was unable to make it to their rendezvous. Their lives have been adrift since that missed meeting. The other interpretation sees their meeting as a fulfillment, a romance no longer deferred but finally culminating in Celine's apartment. And the deferred romance, in this view, is what allows for its success. They didn't grow tired of one another in their early twenties—their boring stories, their ingrained habits. Instead, their romance blooms in absentia.

Over the years in graduate school, I found myself more interested in parties and going out than I'd been since I was twenty-one. My then-wife worked at an office job downtown, dutifully helping the environment, a passion we shared. On some weekends, we saw her parents, drove out to the forest and tossed around frisbees, walked the dog by the shore. I liked that life as well, but I couldn't square these divergent pieces of self, the drinking and dancing and fun with the easy family picnics. I wanted to merge both lives, but the bridge seemed impossible, a step too far. I hid myself. I was ashamed of the way I wanted the things I'd sworn off in college: alcohol, dancing, desire, fun.

How to square the life I already had with the one I could now see? I was living in two places at once: the life I'd missed out on, and the life I was already living. Sometimes, I'd wake up for church at eight, hungover from the night before, living in both realities at once. The pastor would talk about God, the congregation would lift its voices to the heavens, and I'd want to cry, to stop the singing from splitting my hungover head open, to stop it from telling me I had to change my life.

No one in my program was publishing. We were the last group of students to attend an MFA without any sense of why. Our reasons for entering the program grew vaguer to me as time went by. We talked about writing without doing much of it. People complained about the reading lists, about the lack of time for writing, which we all wasted anyway. For years afterward, I gave up writing, too.

After graduate school, my wife and I bought a duplex with a small yard in the far northwest corner of Washington, D.C. The death of my grandmother had left us with enough money for a down payment. My own beloved grandmother, a mirror to the grandmother in the movies, except, instead of keeping us apart, her death allows my wife and I to move forward, out of the life I had been traveling toward in bars, in the absence of God and back into the picture of domestic happiness.

We put up a privacy fence, a small garden with yarrow, vertiginous cone flowers, abundant black-eyed Susans. And then the children, a family, the old American Dream. An older girl, just like I'd always wanted, reed-thin, strong-willed and whip smart. And we stay at home, and nurse her, and care for her, and I read *Curious George* so many times that I want him to die horribly or to throw the book into the Marianna Trench, but I am also enraptured, in love, and when her little body is curled up against mine, both of our skins warm, I am the most content I have ever been, even if it's only for those brief moments. My daughter. My love.

But during those same years, I am working at a library job, shipping books across the country, and it starts to bore me. A new manager takes over our small operation, a petty, mean person, who makes each day at work a living hell. I adore the hours with my daughter, and they also unmake me. What to do with the hours of misery, of disappointment, of boredom that make up so much of my days?

In the afternoons, I print shipping labels, cut them out and spend an hour affixing them to packages, taping and boxing, sending books in manilla envelopes to people who are still dreaming: professors and graduate students, intrepid undergrads. In a way, it's like sending hope in small manilla packages, but it's a hope I've begun to lose for myself.

I belabor a second child, feel that old unhappiness running wild as weeds in a garden. A second child arrives nonetheless, fat and happy. A little bundle of joy. He is delighted by the world and makes small growling noises that sound almost like a dinosaur. Love is multiplied, as is the work.

Parenting is a whir of days. My daughter throws constant tantrums, pees on the floor when we put her on timeout. She insists on wearing frilly dresses. I carry her out of every event we attend over my shoulder as she screams. Whatever romanticism life once carried has been worn away. I settle into unhappiness, start reading Knausgaard's monument to shame and mid-life malaise. In those books, I recognize a mirror to myself, a person unequipped for happiness.

In between the two movies, Hawke and Delpy tried to get funding for a bigger-budget sequel that was to take place in several cities. *Before Sunrise* had been a hit on the indie circuit, but it hadn't made enough money to draw interest for a larger project from a major studio.

It's strange to think what might have been in that imagined sequel. The actual second movie, which clocks in at a mere eighty minutes, is considered by many critics to be the finest in the trilogy. Linklater worked with Hawke and Delpy on the script, filming in a madcap fifteen days. The three writers scrapped the larger script and wrote an entirely new story.

Part of the inspiration for making the film was Hawke's divorce from his long-time wife, Uma Thurman. With the fallout of his marriage fresh, the script is rife with descriptions of a relationship turned from the romantic into the domestic, a sharing of errands and appointments as opposed to connection.

Years later, I read about hedonic adaptation, the psychological wiring of our brains that makes us adapt to our circumstances, get used to whatever was once desired and move to the next thing, a new car, a new house, a nicer armchair or spouse. We forget we have attained what we once desired. Satisfaction eludes us.

But this knowledge is in the future, and it merely confirmed what I felt but could not speak. After the confirmation, what to do with life? How to solve it? At times during my marriage, I find myself thinking of the countryside, of Europe, wishing I could meet someone on a train, a person who has the key to solve this riddle of self that structures my days. I'll chat with people at work, occasionally breaking through the malaise of chatter to have the sort of conversation I've always loved, the brain suddenly firing again, suddenly interested in each twist and turn. And what are these moments telling me? Is it a trap, like the sirens in the *Odyssey?* Or is it the truth of things, that a deeper life is waiting for me elsewhere?

And still, we watched television shows most evenings. We'd chat about our days, sitting in the basement on our tan couch. On weekends, we'd often drive two hours away and spend time with her family, whom I adored, playing Frisbee golf on sand dunes, hiking in swampy parks. I may have sometimes felt distant from that life, but I also wrestled with it. I understood that my life was, by all accounts, good. That we had a good life. I struggled with the battle between the perception of life and what I felt I should perceive.

Every few months, we'd have a big fight, over the fact that I didn't believe in God or that we were never going to travel to Spain. I'd say that our lives were too structured, too planned. That we needed to have more fun. And after these blow-ups, we'd lie on opposite sides of the bed, breathing in the dark. In the morning, we'd pretend like the fight hadn't happened and go back to the daily routines of changing diapers, of scheduling appointments, of choosing a television show for the evening.

In a way, the second movie is about that single night carrying an allure for Jesse and Celine that life doesn't. I recognize that desire in myself, an undefined yearning, and when I don't get what I yearn for, I look inward, look elsewhere, get unaccountably sad for days in ways that don't reflect reality. Life can always be a disappointment if managed in a certain way. My brain is the unlikeable narrator of my own life.

The chemistry between Celine and Jesse is palpable, the attraction of their bodies, now in each others' orbit again after nine years of waiting. As they wander the streets, dipping into a coffee shop to talk about where the time has gone, their attraction builds. Jesse gazes across at Celine at the coffee shop as though she might evaporate if he stops staring. As they walk through a garden and joke about the possibility of the end of the world, Jesse pulls Celine into his lap, says if the world was ending, he'd like to fuck for days.

Then a breakage, an insertion of the real world, Celine, who has known of Jesse's marriage the whole time, suddenly asks him about his wife, his child. A pause in the forward thrust of the narrative, a fracturing of the time that characterizes the second movie. Suddenly, their magical world is no longer entirely theirs. And her question is intentional, a trump card she's carried with her into the day, a reason for her distance. Her question is at once a pause, a censure, and an invitation towards revelation and transgression.

Linklater said the first movie was supposed to be set in a magical time, one dazzling night of connection with a stranger. The second movie is supposed to be set in real time, with the pressures of the world, a flight to catch, a spouse to return to, a child weighing at the periphery, a tight constraint of eighty minutes.

The revelation about Jesse's marriage shifts the tenor of the film. Their affair still seems inevitable, but Jesse's answers to the question of marriage will define how many viewers understand it. For a staunch defender of marriage, one built on mutual fidelity and trust, Jesse can provide no answer that would allow for what's to come. For others, often those who have been at the end of loveless marriages, sleeping on the couch in the basement, myself included, the end will seem inevitable.

At each juncture of their walk, Celine keeps reminding Jesse he will miss his flight, and he keeps begging off, insisting that he can afford ten more minutes, one more boat ride, one more moment with her. She keeps reminding him about the life he has to return to, a wife and a child, and he ignores her each time, insisting on the connection, insisting on making up for all the lost years between them.

On a whim, they board a small boat taking tourists along the Seine. The ship moves slowly, light swims on water, Notre Dame rising in the distance, an Impressionist painting. As Celine walks to the front of the ship, the camera shoots her from behind. Her shirt billows, revealing a pale flash of stomach. Julie Delpy's face is soft and vibrant, and I am in love with this small moment in the film: the boat ride, the façade of Notre Dame, the contingency of the wind, a mirroring of the contingency of life, of the films, of everything.

Sometimes I think the problem I had during those years was my understanding of marriage, which I thought should be so rich with possibility, rich with adventures, rich with experiences. I thought the same of life, of work. I kept looking for the romance I'd been promised, and I couldn't find it in anything at all. I knew it was a fault. I joked about it. I tried to wish it away, but I couldn't make it disappear. I couldn't live with the yearning.

In graduate school, my wife and I take a long trip to Italy to visit my sister, who has married an Italian man and settled in Bologna. We stare in awe at the Colosseum, at the green waters of Venice, wander the back alley in search of rare books, climb the Duomo in Florence, marvel at the Sistine Chapel, share a perfect affogato in a small town overlooking the Ligurian Sea. I still sometimes think of the David by Michelangelo, the marvelous curve of that sculpture. Those weeks together like a dream, marriage once again an adventure, a window into the unknown.

Jesse says that something seems amiss. Even on his wedding day, he was thinking of Celine, of the road not taken. He imagines he sees her sometimes, passing on the street. She later confirms she was in New York that year, studying in the United States. And his whole face droops, the years suddenly arriving all at once, the disappointment and failure.

And the central question, at least for an adult, is whether this chance is worth it or yet another romantic delusion. Should they or shouldn't they? Would they have grown in love or grown tired of one another if they'd married young? Would Jesse have wearied of Celine's fears, her constant badgering? Would Celine have grown tired of Jesse's silly enthusiasm for life, his way of floating above the domestic sphere in the realm of abstraction? What of the unseen marriage?

That Jesse's wife is off-screen, unable to defend herself, feels pertinent, both to the film and to my own attempt at writing about relationships. Hawke's divorce from Uma Thurman pauses me, makes me wonder about how much went into it. What does it mean to Thurman, the real wife, to Jesse's fictional wife, both absent? What does this project mean to the women I write about who are in absentia? This question looms over the entire project herein as it does over the movie.

For the purposes of the film, this absence is key. The viewer feels sorry for the wife, but most are still able to root for Jesse and Celine, their magical connection. If life has unfolded in a certain way, left them older, wiser, sadder, they are still walled off, still in time entirely their own. This is where I'd disagree with Linklater. There are no interruptions, no squalling children, no irritating email from a job. In this walled-off state, infatuation flourishes, and viewers relish it.

Fiction gives us the opportunity to create infinite narratives. But it turns out most of the movies we like best end in one of two ways, romance or loss. It's hard to say what my first wife's story of our marriage would be. In a way, I think she felt betrayed by my constant unhappiness, my chafing at the bonds of a regular family life. She was a perfectionist; our house was clean; our children were well taken care of; our finances were in good shape. How could we not be okay?

I have always been difficult to please, high energy and capricious. I think my unsteadiness made our life together difficult. My desire for adventure was countered by her practicality, and because we both felt the other person was overdoing it, we dug in our heels, complained. And eventually, toward the end, we just gave up and went our separate ways because we could no longer agree on the story of our lives. I was still hungry for more.

In a way, we both wanted control of the narrative. I wanted us to careen through the night like a train off its tracks, and she wanted us to remain steady, to find happiness through the drumbeat of continual good decisions. In her view, this would lead to the best outcomes and maximal freedom. But we couldn't find common ground. We found living hard. We were too young when we got married. We didn't know who we were. We still don't, but the picture is clearer now.

But here is what I remember from before.

I remember a vacation we took before the children, with her father and her brother. I remember the guided tour in Canyon Lands, the red rocks giving way to a slot canyon, where we walked, red rock on the right, a strip of blue sky overhead, but darkness in the canyon. Overhead, crows flew by with bits of an animal, roadkill I suppose, hanging in their claws. I remember their caws, the bright rock, the shadows. What I'm saying is that it's from her and her family that I learned my spirit of adventure. As a child, we'd been too poor to afford any vacations. It was during those years with her that I found a new self.

I remember driving our daughter home, how in the days after her difficult birth, an unplanned C-section, all the trees had lost their leaves, bony fingers stretching into a vault of blue sky and our tender child, pink-faced, drowsing in the backseat. I remember those first few tender weeks when little S would only sleep if we held her in our arms, how she'd wake up screaming each time we tried to put her down in her crib, how we used to watch her so closely, focusing on every little breath, panicking at each hiccup, wondering if she were still alive. And in the intensity of those days, it was as though our marriage was renewed; we had a common goal, to keep the child alive, which bonded us again, pulling toward the same goal with the kind of effort that had eluded us in the intervening years.

I remember lying in bed, just after our son was born, his warm body curled on my chest. I remember my daughter, just two, wild-eyed and questioning. I remember my wife standing in the doorway, her voice full of happiness as she snapped a picture. Winter light through the window, warm bodies in bed.

You're a father of two now.

But the discontent, which has been running like a subterranean river beneath our lives, finally floods everything. In those years of child-rearing, of doctor appointments, of changing diapers, of explosive shit that coats the wall, of tantrums and working nightly to share duties, we lose one another.

We sit on the porch and talk of our unhappiness, the things unspoken through the years, the disappointments, the missed connections, the things we wanted from one another, from our lives, from what we'd been building, and we cry and cry, the children sleeping inside. The porch lights attract insects. We rock back and forth in chairs we swore we'd sit in for decades, staring out into the night beyond. This is maybe the saddest I've been in my whole life. And the insects bump into the light every time my life falls apart.

I can still remember those white chairs, and the way we stared off into the darkness, as though making eye contact would break the spell of our unmaking. We talked for hours and never really talked like that again. A thousand words can't bring it back together, so we say none at all. Our marriage falls apart after that conversation, but we pretend it hasn't, that there is something left to be salvaged, but neither of us is willing to try.

Perhaps I should have said something sooner. Maybe if we'd taken that trip to Spain. Maybe the idea that you're meant to be with someone forever is evil. Maybe I was always trying to live a dream of life: religion, a lovely wife, a perfect family that didn't suit me. Maybe the world doesn't suit me.

I slumber in the basement. The children visit me at night, curl up next to me for a bit and say goodnight, returning upstairs. Even if we haven't decided yet, we've decided. We won't be staying together for the children. Something is cracked, the relationship leaks out everywhere. We unmake things, unmake ourselves.

I move a few blocks away, a trial separation that is really no trial at all. The children's time is divided neatly between the house and my apartment. The conversation with my ex is about the children now, the logistics of summer camp, progress at school, their behavior across the two homes. In the background, I wonder if we've made a mess of their lives. Wonder if they'll be writing about the divorce years later, the imperfections of their two parents. Wonder if they'll write long essays about my abundant failures.

After they leave the Seine, the boat, the intensity of their connection renewed, Jesse and Celine slowly drive toward her apartment for their final parting. On the car ride, Celine has a breakdown. She details the suffering and disappointment she feels in her life and in her romantic relationships. Each failed relationship scars her a little bit more than the last; each time, she feels the loss more acutely. In a way, she says, she blames Jesse and his book, for reminding her of how hopeful she'd once been. She threatens to get out of the car, stares pensively out the window, argues, shouts, mourns the loss of that youthful idealism.

The vulnerability of their conversation opens a space between them, an acknowledgement that the night they shared in Vienna has lingered for both of them. The car stops, and Jesse tells the driver to wait while he takes Celine to her apartment. As they walk into the courtyard, Celine pauses to hug Jesse, and Hawke expertly registers the shock of her lingering hug, his face filled with both surprise and delight at this intimacy.

Jesse walks with her up to her apartment, the two winding up the staircase in silence, not quite catching one another's eyes. It's a visual recreation of their scene in the record store from the first movie, a doubling. Their slow walk, a promise of the intimacy to follow.

Once inside her apartment, Jesse asks Celine to play him a song. She plays a waltz, a surprising song, for the viewer and for Jesse, a song dedicated to their night together so many years before. The two movies and lovers are finally stitched fully together, the yearning, the unlived life, both so painfully real for them.

And when they finally acknowledge they are about to sleep together, it is, as in the first movie, not Jesse's decision. It is Celine who sways her hips and intones, "Baby, you are going to miss that plane." And he leans back, a radiant smile passing over his face. The movie fades to black.

Linklater's films are a strange kind of perfection, but they are also documents of the Anthropocene. The films begin and end with a quick succession of shots of the places Jesse and Celine visit over the course of their walks, but the spaces aren't resonant. Rather, without the presence of humans they are rendered inert, a brief stopping place for the consciousness of the camera, now devoid of meaning. We are just passing through.

The films touch lightly on the decaying infrastructure of global capitalism, cheap labor, environmental degradation, but mostly they are about the intensity of the connection between the two leads. They are more akin to the impressionist paintings or the modernist novels of the early twentieth century, which try to trace what personhood—a particular type of personhood, American and Western European—felt like in the late twentieth and early twenty-first centuries. What was it like to be a feeling, thinking, reasonably well-educated person inhabiting the world? What are the questions raised by marriage, by child-rearing, by the vicissitudes of a life?

And that's what makes the movies an endless source of renewal. They aren't so much movies as snapshots of a moment in time. Even as you can "read" them as cultural products, talk about capitalism, the development of reality television, referenced in the first movie, or the awareness of the United States as a colonial occupier, of large corporations lying and politicians shilling for power, the movies aren't about that. They are about moments of being.

I'd like to have a neat little writing trick to bind up the end of my marriage with the conclusion of the second movie. Readers enjoy narrative continuity. It suggests a particular construction made by an expert. And though the idea appeals to me, it is impossible. A life doesn't unfold on a neat track. And I remain baffled by the oddities, the ship running aground. Jesse divorced and I divorced. We both tried to make life anew.

But first, narrative continuity. The marriage. What to remember from the second movie, an opportunity missed, a chance seized? What to remember of the marriage? The little house and garden? The sunset along the beach, our arms pulling each other into a cinematic kiss. The way all the trees had gone bare at the birth of our daughter. The children, gurgling and laughing on the floor. The children. The children. My God, the children.

I remember a summer when we lived in a condo, mere blocks away from where the Atlantic carved away at the beach. And where, at night, we'd watch the moon lie as a ribbon across the dark bay, gulls carving sky overhead. We worked easy jobs that summer, jobs that took nothing from us. And on Friday evenings, we'd curl up on the couch and watch episodes of *Arrested Development* for hours, laughing, our bodies folded into one another. We were happy that summer.

ACT III

Before Midnight

Mid-life comes for us all. When I was younger, people always said the young made the mistake of thinking they'd live forever. The joke must go, the middle-aged are afraid they *will* live forever. As children age and parents begin to rapidly slow, the opportunities for life narrow, days quicken in their familiarity, so life accelerates toward its natural end at the same time as its churn increases. It can make a person desperate. It can make a person want to unmake a life, to move back into their twenties, to reopen all the doors, to gather the smells from that garden of youth. Any number of mammals seem to suffer from what we'd call a mid-life crisis, the U-curve shape of happiness, and I suppose it's a matter of what we do with it, this feeling of our own unmaking.

The third film, *Before Midnight*, finds Jesse and Celine on vacation in Greece, nine years after their fateful meeting in Paris, twin daughters now in tow. Over the course of the movie, we see a radical corrective to the romance of the first two films. The world, which has been held at bay by the gravitational pull of their connection, is foregrounded.

And it's the world's intrusion that leads the two of them to begin fighting, launching into a monstrous argument that covers their antipathies, housework, childcare, fidelity, Jesse's ex-wife, the sort of exhausting catalog that can be stored over the course of a relationship. The two take their relationship to the brink and peer into the abyss before the final moment when their connection is reestablished, a hint that they will go on together through the imperfections and sadness, arguments and challenges of a long-term partnership.

The core of the third film is the question of what happens when life takes precedence over romance. What was held at bay during their lamplit walk on the Danube and meandering conversation on the Seine is suddenly the real question. What is a marriage and connection against the making of grocery lists, cleaning up after children, arguing over how to discipline the kids or navigate the thorny pathways of a career?

When I first saw the movie in 2013, I recognized the signs of a marriage that had become difficult, my own in the process of being swallowed by an avalanche of dirty diapers, of freezing baby food, of administering the milk at the perfect hour. And beyond that, we had both changed so much from twenty-three and twenty-one, but we hadn't found a way to realign ourselves. The struggle for control was long over, and we were deep in the doldrums.

Many lovers of the first two movies didn't like *Before Midnight*, the last forty minutes of which track a grueling fight in a hotel room. Celine is volcanic and rude, Jesse mean and condescending. Critics, though, mostly loved the movie, praising its authenticity. I think a person's perspective of the movie is largely dependent on whether they go to movies to escape reality or to be confronted by it. By the time I saw *Before Midnight*, I was desperately in need of confrontation.

Every relationship is a mystery to those who aren't at the center of it. We cannot see who washes the dishes after the party, who pays the bills, who tells the jokes to lighten the mood, who goes quiet for spells, dips into a book, thinks about their childhood, a possible lover, the work project looming on Monday. We don't see who throws an arm over a shoulder, offers an apology on the couch, who is the cartographer of days.

Then again, I also sometimes say the only people who truly see a relationship are those who *aren't* in it. From the outside, the patterns of a relationship are clearer. Look at how he always cuts her off mid-story, fails to pick up the kid's toys. See how she controls him, complains of his slovenly t-shirt in front of friends. See how much she laughs when he's away, how he flirts outrageously.

I believe both things are true. Only those who are inside and only those who are outside a relationship can truly understand it, which leaves us with mystery. The human mind prefers rigid order. It has proved useful in the setting of train tracks, in factory schedules, in the digging of canals and making of automobiles. But I think this mania for order fails when confronted by relationships, which, in all their nuances, their baggage, their unseen cracks, defy easy quantification.

My first marriage always looked good from the outside. We were two conventionally attractive, well-educated people who bought a home at the right time, sent out a Christmas card each year, spent time with extended family. There has been a lot of ink spilled on this very subject, the quiet desperation lying underneath the veneer of happiness. But you never feel like your life is a cliché because it isn't. It's your life, gristle and bone. And though I was often frustrated by our life, by our differences, I could never quite say. We were conflict avoidant.

I think others saw this frustration as well. Friends listened to my jokes about the difficulty of marriage and parenting, or how for stretches of time I stopped talking about my marriage at all. They quietly perceived the desperation I thought I was so carefully hiding. It was a secret to no one. After the separation, my mother said she always thought there was something off, something missing. A dear friend of mine said she thought that I always seemed like I thought I should be happy but wasn't.

I don't quite know what story to believe. I believe that we were very young. I believe that we once traveled to Italy, marveled at the majesty of the David. I believe that we often had the best of intentions even as we began to fall apart. I believe that it was a difficult match, two people who both desperately wanted control—of time, of vacations, of finances—and who found it hard to compromise over and over again in the harsh light of marriage. I think, had we been older—twenty-eight, thirty—we probably would have drifted apart without getting married. But we were also once young and in love, and we couldn't see the future; we could only see each other, barely twenty, imagining a life. Beyond that, what constitutes a failure in a relationship? What's a success? I'll leave it for the Puritans and the moralists.

After the separation, I was quickly involved in another relationship. Everyone says the important thing to do after the end of a relationship is to take time to yourself, to meditate, to walk, to think about what you want in the next phase of your life. It's good advice, but rarely taken. Relationships are as familiar as breathing.

Before Midnight hinges on the sort of fight therapists say you should avoid. It's a roving argument that isn't about any one thing. Instead, it's about everything that frustrates Jesse and Celine about the other person. They engage in character assassinations, question one another's fidelity, motives, integrity. Celine is ready to burn everything to the ground during the fight, consistently saying their relationship has run its course.

At first, things went well with my new partner. We had wonderful conversations, an intense connection that had been missing. The laughter, the joy in discovering another person's thoughts, were suddenly a daily part of my existence again. In this relationship, I was called out for my doldrums, my glum outlook on life. I was reminded that most people like me, that I'm genuinely fun, interested and interesting, that I've misunderstood my life.

One afternoon, we get a pizza from a nearby restaurant, then wander around the gorgeous houses in Cleveland Park—old trees, broad porches—and into the woods, where we discover a small sanctuary of grass behind the massive houses. Mid-meal, she begins rolling down the hill, laughing exuberantly, carelessly, an embodiment of the letting go I've been waiting a lifetime for.

And yet, the intensity of the connection, which I always thought I wanted, begins to drive us apart. Quickly enough, we come to our point of intransigence, being in different life circumstances and unable to agree on a route forward. Still, we held on. And what else to do then but argue?

Most couples fight at least once or twice a month. Whether it's over finances, the behavior of the kids or work, disagreement is inevitable. But it's the way the argument flows as a river through an old valley that determines the happiness of the couple: which channels are followed, which abandoned. Happy couples tend to argue about problems they can solve, as opposed to those issues that are intransigent.

A fight can be like a black hole, pulling everything into its event horizon.

We argued over nearly everything. The quality of Michael B. Jordan's acting in *Black Panther*. Time travel logistics in the television show *Dark*. The sadness in the essays I was publishing. My not-yet-finalized divorce, and my not-yet-ex-wife. How I was raising the children. The fighting should have burned us out quickly, made us realize we weren't a good fit. But we kept returning to one another, kept giving things one more try. We talked about therapy, about the children, about the ways we could change.

We downloaded a podcast and listened to a pair of therapists talk about the handling of strong emotions. I finally started therapy after years of recommendations from friends. I discussed the dissolution of the marriage, my loss of belief in God, in purpose, in the romantic idealism of youth, my father. I read Thich Nhat Hanh's book *On Anger*.

The relationship lasted for years, difficult years, strange years, years that feel almost unreal now. My life slowly unraveling at the same time I swore I was holding everything together, swore that I was trying my best, even as I wasn't, even as I went abroad, slept with a stranger, did everything to say that I was not ready for a relationship and yet remained in one. In retrospect, I see those years as me trying to enact a corrective, to justify the ending of my marriage with the success of this relationship. The issue could not have been me, and this new relationship allowed me to forego the blame, the questioning, the doubts.

My new partner and I traveled to Italy as I'd done during my marriage, a chance at starting over, a way to both relive and improve upon the memory. But the flight over was a disaster of delays and cancelations, Italy becoming more of a mirage than a place we'd eventually reach. We stalked through airports, hissed at one another in London, wandered around like zombies trying to find plugs for our phones.

When we arrived in Italy, I realized I'd forgotten to bring my license, and the woman at the counter said we couldn't have the rental car. We sat on a wall, deflated, exhausted, wondering if the trip would ever begin or if we'd sit here forever, in limbo.

We stood in line again and got a different clerk, one who quickly helped us, added a second driver, and we were off into the small roads beyond Rome, towns built on the hillsides shining above us in the Umbrian countryside. Who could be miserable in all this glory?

We drove into the hills, climbed the narrow roads into the cities mounted on the Tufa. As we walked the streets, we paused to admire bougainvillea climbing a house, purple flowers blooming on stone. But the misery consumed us again. One of us would go silent, and the other would become annoyed at the silence, pry at it, seeking to shake the other out of their lethargy. We were both so attuned to the slightest shift in moods that it was nearly impossible to be around one another. I drank a glass of wine and ate pasta in a small bar while we argued. On the television, Roger Federer choked away set points against Novak Djokovic.

Annoyed, we parted ways, leaving one another to explore this marvel of a city alone. I walked to the edge of town, gazed out on the valley splayed out below, fields awash in golden light, the foreground swathed in darkness from the hill on which I stood. The streets behind me were narrow and dark between the houses, cobblestones aglow in the sunlit square, an ornate cathedral pinning blue skies.

In the beauty, I lost track of my anger, watched it dissipate as fog burning off a hillside. I wandered farther, out to the edge of town where I could look more closely at the tufa, the soft bedrock formed from volcanic ash that is why these hill towns exist. A geologic anomaly. As the bedrock of our childhoods, our parents, our old lovers, our choices, form the bedrock of the anomalies we are, too.

I felt something gathering in me with the force of a storm, a pure desire to be alone. The feeling had been growing in me of late, a desire to gather in the world without the obstruction of another person, someone who I had to frame things for. For so long, all I'd wanted was connection, and now I was slowly realizing I wanted mostly to be alone, unfettered, wandering by myself.

After I gathered the small illuminations on my iPhone I went back to the square to find her. I showed her a picture I'd taken, the gleaming steps, a bright cathedral, a row of cumulus clouds above. I wanted to show her that beauty could make things better, but I said nothing at all. We drove back toward our hotel in the Umbrian countryside, the valleys slowly being swallowed by night.

In the first two movies, the camera neatly follows Jesse and Celine, tracing their meandering path through Vienna and

Paris. The third movie intentionally complicates this choice, beginning with an iconic shot from the first movie, two pairs of shoes walking side by side. However, this time it isn't Jesse and Celine, but Jesse's son who walks alongside him as they trace a path to the airplane that will take him back to his mother, Jesse's ex-wife. The father and son relationship is a casualty of the choice Jesse makes by choosing Celine, and the movie opens with their conversation, with Jesse's pain at missing the important moments in his son's life. Already, the real world has gone from abstraction to reality.

After his son boards the plane, it's Jesse's sadness at his son leaving, at the distance between them, that becomes a catalyst for the fight between he and Celine. They argue over whose career will take precedence, how often they'll see his son if they move back to America.

There is a quiet sadness, at least for a romantic, watching Jesse and Celine behaving as a married couple—harried, haggling, as they drive through the Greek countryside. As they drive, Celine shares a story from her childhood and Jesse is shocked because it's a story he hasn't heard before. In the first two movies, Jesse was attuned to everything Celine said, every story a new discovery. The movie is careful to depict these moments, to show how much familiarity shifts our romantic relationships, and makes them more like a partnership.

Many people predicted the pandemic would lead to divorces, as couples were forced to spend constant time together and, in the process, discovered how truly unhappy they were. Interestingly, that supposition didn't prove true. In fact, a study by Bowling Green University revealed a twelve percent decline in divorces for 2020. By removing the outside world, most relationships actually improved. Most people, it turns out, don't dislike their spouses so much as they dislike the endless petty tasks, the commute and laundry and meetings that could have been emails—all the ways that life in the twenty-first century is deeply alienating to a sense of being in and belonging to the world.

We all wonder how relationships are supposed to turn out. Are humans supposed to be monogamous? How do you tell when a relationship has run its course? What makes a couple thrive while another falls? Connection? Independence? How is it possible a person can be reviled in one relationship and adored in the next?

Before Midnight, like most interesting works of art, doesn't answer these questions directly. Instead, at a dinner party in the home of a famous writer, various couples share their views on marriage and relationships. The youngest couple at the table, though in love, acknowledges their long-term relationship won't last due to distance and jobs. They say they are but a passing moment in one another's life. The middle-aged couple spars, jokes, ironizes their relationship, annoyed and enraptured by one another. They imply they are stuck together. The oldest man, the writer who invited Jesse, says he and his wife have always been individuals, free to pursue their lives together and apart, which is why she hasn't been with them for most of the month of Jesse's residency.

The differing views are not intended to clarify marriage or long-term relationships but to complicate them. The way forward is never defined for you, never entirely clear, but a mixture of cultural, social, and personal choices. And the thing to find is not someone else's vision for marriage or partnership but your own.

The most moving portrait at the dinner table comes from the lone single person, a widow, who recounts the little mannerisms she misses about her husband, the way he'd whistle on the street, his comments about the weather. All those little details that make him human, an echo of Celine from the prior movie. As the older woman talks, the rest of the table sits in silence, listening carefully. I did, too. My romantic soul, it seems, is not yet gone.

The woman says she still tries to remember every detail of her husband's face, to bring him back into being. But then she says the world rushes back in, and he's gone again. She says that he appears and disappears. "Just like our life—we appear and we disappear and we are so important to some, but, we are just passing though."

What to make of the years? After a lovely morning of reading and writing, my wife asks how I am doing. Meh, I answer. I think I need something else. I am such a contingent creature. Aren't we all? If only I could create a contiguous self, one who could inhabit those memories of new parenthood, of love, a river covered in ice, a cardinal perched on an ever-green above a snowy floor, or my son tucked beneath my right arm as we snooze just after his birth. Time is the enemy.

Why write an essay about your romantic and personal failures? They're all I've got.

And here the narrative begins to break down, right when I'd like it to be building momentum as a train finally leaving the city, entering into the wide-open countryside. The neat connection I'm trying to impose between my rela-tionships and the movies. But I cannot hold together the insides anymore, and they begin to bleed together. Memory layered upon memory as a Roman church built on the ruins of a pagan temple.

An essay is like a jigsaw puzzle, an arrangement of memories, which my neurons have stored for some purpose I can't always divine. Perhaps all I'm saying is I have always loved romantic gestures, the idealistic flourish. Montaigne, the first and greatest essayist, I do not try to portray being: I portray passing.

We are all just quicksilver light piercing the trees, here and then gone. And my mind clings desperately, as barnacle to rock, to the past. The first time I kissed someone I was nineteen years old, standing beneath a row of trees, boughs as antlers, the moon keeping silent vigil.

The argument in *Before Midnight* raises provocative and familiar questions about the nature of marriage. Whose pro-fessional dream is pursued? How are the duties of childcare, meal planning and cooking split between two partners? Is fidelity the key marker of what makes a relationship function? Is it long-lasting commitment? Love? Respect?

These questions aren't explicitly answered by the third movie, but the resolution, the two of them sitting outside, a sliver of hope, the sea gone dark in the distance, suggests something. The answer, at least according to the movie, seems to be in the commitment to live with the other person, to accept or at least tolerate their faults in order to remain together. To witness them, in all their foibles and pleasures, and not turn away.

But it would be misreading the movie to say it's only that. Jesse and Celine clearly still enjoy one another, make each other laugh, make each other think. The chemistry between the two characters is still the central tenet that binds them. Perhaps it's sufficient to be committed and enjoy one another? To take joy, pleasure. To not slip into the darkness.

After my girlfriend and I leave Tuscany, we drive to the Amalfi coast. The narrow roads, so beautiful when shot from overhead on Instagram with drones, are hellish to drive on. The day before, we'd been to Pompeii, where we witnessed the bodies encased in ash, the wildflowers growing in what once were kitchens and living rooms. Everything passes. Down an old path, made wildly uneven by the passage of time, the earth's pitch and yaw, we see a long row of bodies gathered in the darkness, waiting to be moved to museums in southern Italy or studied by archeologists, two thousand years waiting. In the distance, Vesuvius looms, bones of the dead jutting up in memory, like an accordion playing the light.

In Amalfi, we stay on the coast, an apartment with a view of the sea. In the morning, we try to hike down an old trail to the coast. But the trail is vicious, steep stone steps, which are hell on the knees, and the hike seems to go on forever. We leave the trail and walk the narrow, sidewalk-less roads instead. Buses full of tourists zip by. Eventually we make our way into Amalfi, but we're surprised to find it dingy, run down. The beaches are stone, and it's a few bucks to rent a towel. Inside the city, there are overpriced snow cone shops and chintzy jewelry. My partner says it reminds her of Jersey. Briefly, we turn our annoyance toward the place, one more tourist trap.

We take the harrowing bus ride home, inching along the switchbacks. I assure her everything will be fine, that these trips are taken fifty times a day. As we grind our way up, the driver pulls over, stops the bus and hops out. He begins smoking a cigarette. For five minutes, the whole bus waits. Finally, someone asks him what's wrong, and he gestures to the wheel, which is starting to come loose from the well. We wait for an hour on the side of the road, the bus driver casually blowing smoke into the breeze. We are miserable in Italy.

Back in our apartment, we wonder if we should drive to Rome, leave the mess of cheap beaches, rickety buses and overpriced snow cones of Amalfi behind. After a back and forth, we settle on staying to attend a dinner I've booked, and we drive out toward Positano, car hugging ever-narrowing roads. On one sharp turn, I slam on the brakes and a truck passes us, three large trees loosely tied to its top; their trunks sway over us as the truck turns. When I try to turn into the lot, the car stalls, and I lay my head down on the wheel, then get out of the car and say I'm done. I get back in the car finally and gun it up the steep grade into the parking lot, my heart pounding. I get out of the car again and say, "That was one of the worst experiences of my life."

As we eat dinner for the next two hours, I'll see couple after couple, many in their seventies, making their way up the steps. Those same drivers navigating those same roads without an ounce of stress.

The dinner is at a family-run winery, with cellars dug on the property, which we visited at the beginning of our trip, standing in the cool well, sipping wine and chatting to our host. At dinner we're the only guests, and the host is gregarious. They have a restaurant on-site, but we've booked a special visit. It's like *Eat, Pray, Love*, except we don't like each other, and I'm mostly looking forward to the drinking. In the cave, the proprietor, a handsome young Italian man, pulls a bottle of wine from a chilly well they've dug, pours us a glass in the musty darkness.

Outside, he starts our meal with fresh figs and a sparkling white. We sit on the hills of Positano, gazing out over the infinity of the sea. Near us, the proprietor roasts figs, goat cheese, wraps them in basil and brings us bottle after bottle of wine. The sun sets over the Ligurian Sea, a riotous pink, clouds dark overhead, the sea a soft purple. The sunset lasts an hour as we eat and drink fresh food, the light refracted through our wine glasses. It's the sort of moment one dreams of—the sea, the sky, the soft cheese melting around the figs.

The proprietor says we can stay the night, offers us a place on his property to crash. I think of when we'll have this opportunity again, sleeping on a small family farm in the hills above the sea. We can drink all night and sleep it off the next day. The romantic choice.

But my partner doesn't want to, fears we'll make a mess of things, miss our trip to Rome. I give up on the romance, and we drive home on the narrow highway, which skirts the houses as it winds through small villages.

On the drive, we get in a riotous argument that lasts until morning. The details evade me, but it seemed we both knew things were over, and we were biding our time in Italy. Back to our apartment, the sea dark, Amalfi and the coastal towns, a mirror of the sky, lights dimly falling from the cities, a small array of color in that ever branching dark.

In *Before Midnight,* as the fight in the hotel room careers, accusations flying, it's hard not to think the romance has gone awry. Who the hell would want that? But the third movie hinges on perception, as perhaps does my view of my own relationships. Whose story is being told?

Whether the viewer thinks Jessie and Celine are a happy couple experiencing a marital blip or an unhappy couple flying down a pathway towards destruction depends on your perception of the fight and of marriage. Thus, the viewer is placed in precisely the same position as Jesse and Celine, who, as they fight, can't seem to get their marriage fully into view. Each person thinks they have been aggrieved, been wronged, been in the right.

This reality is evident even before the fight has started. At the front desk, a clerk recognizes Jesse and asks him to sign her copy of his book. The clerk then asks Celine to sign, too, saying she must be the woman in the story. Initially, Celine refuses, says she's not really in the books, that they are a product of Jesse's imagination. She refuses to co-sign his version of their story.

It was such a pleasure to be immersed in the majesty of Rome. For what is life but a collection of ruins, dreams deferred, hopes quenched, and Rome is the deferred dream made manifest. When I walk through the Forum, witness the spot of Caesar's assassination, the broken columns to a once-great theater of Apollo, it is not with a historian's eye that I see it, standing among the olive trees on Palatine looking down into the empty streets, but as a monument to the hubris of those dreams, to think that anything could last.

It's my second trip to Rome with a partner, another time spent gazing at the wonder of Trevi Fountain, wandering down the Spanish steps at night, sitting with the teens, lounging and listening to live music. The city of *La Dolce Vita*, of the modern masterpiece, *The Great Beauty*. Films

that capture the contingency of life, its random illuminations, little explosions of beauty amidst the mundane.

We argue and eat our pasta in silence. Ever the martyr,
I set out to drink the full bottle of wine myself, a sparkling
Lambrusco I'd first read about in an essay from *Best American
Travel Writing*. The wine goes down easily. A warmth fills
me. I inhabit myself, ignore my partner.

In the street, children scatter in the lanes, parents chatter to one another, all in a language we can't understand.
For years, we've argued over the prospect of having children.
I already have two of my own and feel a growing sense of
unease at the prospect of more: the sleepless nights, the
sheer intensity of bringing another human into the world.
Whenever I'm alone, I feel the strong sense of time being
channeled once more into the grueling hours of wiping bot-
toms and cleaning spit-up. I drink more.

"Are we really just going to sit in Rome having a meal
in silence?"

In *Before Midnight*, Celine asks Jesse if he remembers the
letter he wrote to himself when he was twenty. Yes, he says,
"Jesse, I hope you are not divorced." I made the same promise to myself after my childhood. I, too, failed.

On the day we celebrate my fortieth birthday, the relationship ends, and I enter mid-life, divorced and alone, living
in a dingy apartment. I see my children half the time, but
I also see in myself the vague silhouette of my father before

me. A life I swore I'd avoid. I stare out the window of my apartment onto the street below: idle shopping carts, plastic bags blowing in the breeze. Not even the majesty of Rome in the ruin of life.

The Pulitzer Prize-winning critic Wesley Morris says *Before Midnight* is a movie about the questions that aren't supposed to be asked in a marriage.

The first time I watched the third movie, I was beginning to question my marriage. Thus, the wide-ranging fight between Jesse and Celine about work, parenting, anxiety, ambition, and fidelity, struck me as deeply real, a survey of all the things that go unsaid in order to hold together the edifice of a marriage. Some critics called the movie near-perfect, a realization of something they saw in their own lives. My spouse and I were conflict avoidant, though, more content to pass through the days than to fight over them.

By the time I've seen the movie for the fifth time, my life has shifted again. I no longer see the film as something sad and portentous. Instead, it feels like cleaning out the basement or making a long-overdue visit to the dentist. I don't quite believe in fights, but I no longer believe burying conflict makes a relationship function. Nor do I think every gesture must be analyzed, every stone unturned.

What feels important is that two people remain "interested" in one another. I no longer see every relationship as needing to perform the same function as mine. There is something contiguous about the characters of Jesse and

Celine across the eighteen years of the movie. They have both become more themselves, and it's easier to see them in the third movie. She is a volcanic personality, always jumping ahead to worst-case scenarios, and Jesse balances her out. He is an endlessly curious and seeking person, someone who would be easily bored in the confines of a typical life, and Celine's personality, her pettiness, her flashes of genius, her shit-giving, keeps him on his toes. In short, it's possible to see how these two might function as a couple. Imperfectly? Yes. But that is why the third movie exists, to give an accurate picture of how a marriage between two strong personalities might work.

And it's a pleasure to watch Hawke and Delpy inhabit these characters a third time. Only *Boyhood* and soap operas aim to show the continuity of a singular character across such a large span of time. And that's a joy of the movie, to watch the circumstances of life shift, big decisions get made without a fundamental shift in character. They are both, for all of the thousands of changes, the same two people who said hello to each other on a train.

The movie, and the trilogy, ends with the two of them finally making amends. Jesse writes Celine a letter from herself in the future. In the letter, the future Celine tells herself not to miss this night on the Peloponnesian coast. And Celine, after initial resistance, joins Jesse in his fantasy one more time. The camera fades out, the two of them sitting by the wine-dark sea, the moon overhead. Struggle. Hope.

Forty-two, married again and reflecting on the films, I quote something from the third movie. My wife leans over and asks if the character of Jesse is based on me or if I based myself on him. I tell her I don't know. It seems impossible to know the degree to which I understood myself through the prism of the films, but I find traces of myself laced throughout. I wouldn't be so silly as to base myself on a movie, or maybe that's exactly what I'd do. Maybe that's why, for a period of years, I kept meeting people on trains, on bus rides and on planes, searching for a reproduction of the romance I'd loved when I was a teen. Maybe the self I'd been searching for was aspirational all along, a character in a movie.

But I noticed something strange while thinking about these movies again. An insight I hadn't had before. My partners had always compared me to Jesse, his seeking nature, his curiosity, his desire to write, his abstractions. And whether they found Jesse charming, annoying, or interesting seemed to have a lot to say about the state of our relationship. Now, finally, I'd found someone who found him as interesting as I did.

In between the end of my long-term relationship and meeting L, I went on dates. A lot of dates. Around a hundred or so in nine months. It was a cacophony of humanity, online conversations about whether I wanted to have children, whether I wanted an open relationship, whether I wanted to be a third in a marriage, a parent to other children, whether I wanted to go camping every weekend or go shopping at upscale places by the water. Date after date after date. Conversation after conversation. The whole messy array of humanity, and the whole messy array of self on riotous display.

It was an experience I'd been waiting for my whole life, the chance to try on hundreds of different selves. Each day, each new match was another opportunity to build a new architecture of identity. The very thing my previous partner had disliked about me, my vicissitude, was no longer a problem, but a strength. I grew up in California. I loved the east coast, hiking, coffee shops, long conversations, talking about parenting, about marriage, grabbing three drinks and seeing where the night took us.

Finally, there was a chance to have the inner chaos matched by outer circumstances. And, in those long conversations, on those coffee dates by the water, on those drinks with the sun setting over the Potomac, planes overhead making ribbons in the sky, I began to learn how to love the multitude of selves I'd thought for so long were a problem. When a woman criticized me for a small bit of flour that had fallen out of a bag and onto the floor of my car, I realized we weren't for one another. My flaws were suddenly so openly on display, there was ghosting, call outs, the whole nine yards, and I finally began to trust that the ebullience, the chaos, the whirring mind was me, not some design flaw. Love it or leave it. This a mantra, less to any future partner, and more to myself, the doubts I'd been carrying all these years.

The fist time I met L, we had a quiet date at a bookstore, a date I wasn't even sure was a date. She'd reached out to me via Twitter, and I thought it might just be to meet a local writer. When I arrived, I saw her, a spray of freckles, a soft, pretty face. Maybe it should be a date, I thought. It was November and cold. The wire table was coated in a thin mist. I ordered a cappuccino and started talking.

We talked about dating, about our marriages, and about writing. She shivered through the whole meal. It was her son's birthday, and he was away with her ex. I was still unsure of what it was. A date? A good conversation? When the check came, she said we should split it and meet again soon. When she messaged me again, days later, I understood that it had been a date.

When we met the second time, I drank too much, prattled on about Buddhism, about God, about divorce. In the distance, the dark Potomac. Across the table, L leaning toward me, her face soft, attentive, our conversation fluid, open. I didn't know then what would become of us, but I told her on that date, half-drunk, that I would never be anything but myself and she smiled, said she already liked that about me.

"That's all any of us truly want, to be fully known and still fully loved."

I don't know if the *Before* movies are over or not. There are rumors Delpy was unhappy with the writing credits for the early movies, which failed to cite the immense influence she had. She has toyed with retiring from the movie business altogether after struggling to get her own movie made. In a way, it's easy to see the youthful idealism of Delpy mirroring that of Celine, slowly becoming more disenchanted after the disappointments, not just of life, but of those particular to a woman, in a world and industry still struggling to adapt to the presence of women and other under-represented voices.

Unlike on previous viewings, I no longer recognize the contours of what I want in a relationship from the *Before* movies. Freedom, yes. Intellectual stimulation, absolutely. But the fierce struggle? The idea that a relationship must be constantly fought for? Perhaps it is the lethargy of middle age, but I can't muster the energy any longer. All the indignities of existence seem too much a struggle to add relationship struggles as well. I'd like that part to be relatively easy, as long as the rest is so damn hard. And with L, it is. Our lives are tumultuous in certain ways—ferrying four children around town, mortgage payments, petty squabbles: these are the way we spend our days, so I am happy we are easy with each other.

In his searching essay on pleasure, joy, and sorrow, Ross Gay touches on a moment in *The Great Beauty*, the Italian film that is a logical successor to Fellini's *La Dolce Vita*, about an aging writer who never leaves the scenes and parties in Rome. In the sequences from the film Gay describes, the writer, Jep, walks through an artist's display of endless photos, one for every day of his life. As Jep scans the wall, the music soars, and you see the artist shifting from a child into a man and then drifting into middle age. Jep doesn't say anything, but you can see he's moved by the exhibit, and viewers are moved as well. As Gay puts it, the movie reminds us of the essential factor that perhaps makes life worth living, which is that it ends.

So maybe it's fine there will be no fourth *Before* movie. Nothing lasts in perpetuity. Not a relationship, not Rome, not anything at all. Maybe that's the story of this essay. The small glimmers of things, the meteors flashing across a desert sky, a first kiss, a train ride to Venice, a child's hand smeared in blackberries. This, too, a life. A mere snapshot in time. Maybe I'll write it again when I'm eighty, or maybe I'll have nothing left to say, no story worth telling.

I have lost something, though, with the end of the trilogy marking an end to the relationship between Jesse and Celine. The three movies have served as a guide of what I could expect from the future. At fifteen, I knew one day I'd ride around trains in Europe, discuss religion and philosophy with an intelligent and lovely woman, that my provincial upbringing didn't have to be a terminus in exploring the boundaries of the self. With the second movie, I learned that life and love would have their way with you, that the world has no interest in your happiness, that even love can be a trap, one more disappointment, depending on how you perceive it.

And yet, there would be these little illuminations, the sort Virginia Woolf pursued, the ephemeral and meaningful: a dinner with friends, laughter deep into the evening, a walk through the ruins in Athens or in a small town in Portugal. The world may not be interested in our happiness, but we could still be interested in the world, in short walks with the children, planting bulbs in the fall, hoping for renewal, in repairing relationships even to that lost self, as a potter might a cracked vessel.

The days flit by now, dishwasher full of the scatterings of dinner, of lunch, of the chaos of days. Now the children fill the house again, four of them some days, a riot of voices and elbows and need. How to explain what if feels like to put on the couch cushions, to haggle over the vegetables, to straighten the painting, to sit, some afternoon, when the winter light paints a hallway into the bedroom, brightening the white comforter, while I lie underneath, reading a book, a faint knock at the door. "Dad?"

All of this lies outside the analytic framework of this essay, which attempts to bring order to the raw fragmentation of days. So, I suppose, this whole project is a failed attempt, so much left behind in the churn of days. What does it feel like to be alive? Ineffable.

The dirty old Tiber snakes through Rome. We pause by the postcards, snap pictures of one another, of the distant dome of Saint Peter's Basilica. A row of pigeons strut through the streets. It happened, or something like it, multiple times in my life, even if those memories have faded. And now I've tried to jigsaw it together. In the end, the movie fades to darkness, and I suppose that's the end for all of us.

But we are incandescent in between.

For now, let me dream for a bit while I look out the window of this train at the countryside passing by—the land gone flat, sky rich with clouds, jagged mountains framed in the distance. The key, I keep reminding myself, is not to look outside at the world, at a pretty face, a tree full of crows, expecting it to do anything at all with whatever hunger still lies inside me. The key is to not run everything through the warrens of the self. The world is just the world. The self is just a train passing through the countryside. You don't need to grasp anything at all.

The tracks blur. The countryside passes by, a stand of trees, ragged edge of sky. I look up from a book and away from the countryside rolling past and toward L, reading a draft of this manuscript.

What did you think of the essay?

She looks up. Our eyes meet. Time hurtles through us, no map for the future. She smiles.

ABOUT THE AUTHOR

Andrew Bertaina is the author of the essay collection *The Body Is a Temporary Gathering Place* (Autofocus, 2024) and the short-story collection *One Person Away From You* (Moon City Press Award Winner, 2021). He lives in the D.C. metro area, where he's a lecturer in the English department at American University.

www.ingramcontent.com/pod-product-compliance
Lightning Source LLC
Chambersburg PA
CBHW022032090426
42741CB00007B/1029